Start Investing in Real Estate

Start Investing in Real Estate

From rental income to long-term growth — a practical guide for first-time property investors

Elias Wren

Mindful Pages

Published in 2025

ISBN: 9789371778688 (PB)
ISBN: 9789371779586 (eBook)

Published by

Mindful Pages
Imprint of Alpha Editions LLC
312 W. 2nd St #1834
Casper, WY 82601, USA

This book was developed using advanced writing tools to support the drafting and ideation process. All content has been thoughtfully curated, refined, and reviewed to ensure quality and relevance.

Content

Introduction
The First Brick Is Yours

Property. It is among the oldest expressions of wealth we know—predating banks, predating stocks, even predating money in its modern form. Before pensions and portfolios, there was land: somewhere to live, to cultivate, to raise children, to defend, and eventually to hand down. Yet in today's digitised, high-speed economy, real estate is too often flattened into a mere line item—another entry on a spreadsheet, another trending hashtag in the financial echo chamber.

This book refuses that reduction.

Real estate cannot be understood only in terms of square footage or rental yield. Nor is it merely a nostalgic relic or a shortcut to sudden wealth. At its strongest, it is a long-form statement about identity and values. To buy property—whether that means a modest flat, a weathered duplex, a plot at the edge of town, or units in a trust—is to make a decision about more than finance. It is a declaration of legacy, a choice to stake something tangible in the world. You are not just crunching numbers; you are driving a stake into the ground.

And the first brick is yours.

This is not a manual on flipping houses or a tedious catalogue of tax codes and formulas. Nor will it insult you with the tired mantra of "location, location, location." What you hold here is at once practical, psychological, and philosophical: a guide written for first-time investors who may not have deep pockets but do have intent. It speaks to the teacher with £5,000 tucked away who longs for stability; to the tradesperson thinking beyond next month's wage; to the renter from a younger generation told, endlessly, that the ladder has been kicked away. And it addresses the sceptic too—the one who suspects that property has no place in a future dominated by crypto and AI.

Let's admit it: property today can appear intimidating. Prices have soared, cities are reshaped, and media narratives divide the world into two caricatures—you either belong to the already wealthy insiders, or you've missed your chance entirely. Both claims are false. What remains true is that property offers something no other asset does: tangibility. A door that opens. A patch of earth underfoot. A street that weaves into your story. And perhaps most vital of all, a foundation—material and metaphorical—on which to construct a life.

But a foundation is never laid accidentally.

What lies ahead is not a secret formula. Instead, these pages offer structures of thought, questions to wrestle with, and strategies to approach property as a steward rather than a speculator. Because at its core, real estate is not transactional. It is transformational.

The journey begins not with mortgages or graphs but with mindset. Before stepping into a viewing or pencilling out the figures, you must ask: what kind of investor am I becoming? That requires examining your own beliefs about money, your appetite for risk, your definition of wealth. Chapter One peels back the noise: what is true wealth in a volatile, virtual age? Why does brick and soil still matter when the economy races ever faster into the digital?

Chapter Two turns to practicalities. You do not need a fortune to begin. What you need is clarity, creativity, and the courage to start small. Perhaps you partner with someone you trust. Perhaps you "hack" your own home. Perhaps you explore unconventional paths into the market. Momentum begins not with scale but with intent.

From there, the spectrum of strategies unfolds. Are you the long-term holder who values the quiet compounding of rental income? The renovator who thrives on transformation? Or the contrarian curious about raw land? Chapter Three helps align your method with not only your financial goals but also your temperament.

But tactics alone cannot weather the emotional surges of property. Chapter Four addresses psychology: the fear of making that first offer, the sting of walking away from what seemed perfect, the discipline required when excitement clouds judgement.

Only then do we turn fully to money. Chapter Five looks beyond the simplistic advice of "save a deposit." It explores financing, the true cost of borrowing, the wise use of credit. Real estate has elevated as many people as it has undone. The goal is not entry at any cost, but sustainable participation.

And what makes a good deal? Chapter Six argues it is not always the cheapest property or the highest yield. By weighing three lenses—numbers, neighbourhood, and narrative—you learn to discern true value. You will also guard against deal fatigue, that dangerous impatience that leads to poor choices.

Ownership itself is another threshold. Chapter Seven explores making property perform: cash flow, tax advantages, the systems that allow your investment to serve you rather than enslave you. Not an accountant's manual, but a blueprint for alignment with your larger financial life.

Then comes the human dimension. Chapter Eight speaks of tenants, contractors, neighbours—and your own energy. Boundaries, hiring, delegation: these are as essential as mortgage rates.

Finally, Chapter Nine looks forward. Protection, succession, and legacy. How do you ensure that what you build lasts beyond you? How do you pass on not just square metres but values?

Real estate is never only about property. It is about agency. The ability to shape your environment, to influence your financial path, to secure your future. In an age defined by abstraction, something tangible—walls, earth, a roof—remains an anchor to the real.

And yet, every legacy begins awkwardly. Perhaps you are uncertain, stretched thin, or haunted by past mistakes. That is natural. What matters is not flawless beginnings, but beginnings at all.

You do not need to be fearless. You do not need omniscience. You need only the decision that creating something with your hands, your head, and your heart matters more than waiting endlessly for perfection.

Wealth is not simply accumulated with money. It is shaped with intent.

So, make the first move. The first viewing. The first phone call to a broker. The first conversation with a partner. The first budget scribbled on paper. Lay down the first brick.

Not because it is easy. But because it matters.

Welcome to *Start Investing in Real Estate*. Let us build something meaningful—together.

Chapter 1
Rethinking Wealth, Rethinking Real Estate

Wealth no longer carries the weight it once did. What was once bound up in land, lineage, and permanence has grown curiously fleeting—reduced in many circles to numbers glowing faintly on a screen. Today, value is measured in velocity: how quickly an asset rises, how swiftly it can be flipped, how fast it captures attention. In this digitised economy—where code defines assets, algorithms execute trades, and ownership is abstracted into tokens—the very idea of property can appear stubbornly old-fashioned. Too slow. Too tangible. Too… real.

And yet, it is precisely for those reasons that it endures.

To see why property still matters—perhaps more than ever—we must look past the narrow frame of transaction. Real estate is not merely a financial tool. It is a cultural anchor. It ties us to place, to memory, to identity. While markets spike and collapse, while technologies remake themselves in endless cycles, property persists as one of the few forms of wealth that remains grounded in the human need for space, continuity, and care.

Wander through the winding streets of an old city—Lisbon, London, Kyoto—and you'll encounter the long memory of real estate. Roads carved by centuries of use, façades weathered yet enduring, homes passed down or divided, restored or abandoned. Each doorway holds more than bricks and mortar; it holds decisions. Someone once built it, someone else repaired it, another neglected it. Ownership becomes an archive of human intent. When a flat in a newly fashionable quarter sells for millions, what is changing hands is not just a set of keys but the accumulated story of those who came before. To own property, then, is to step into something larger than oneself. It is less a wager on market movements and more a pledge of belonging.

Yet many modern investors treat property as just another ticker symbol—a box to be ticked, tracked, and offloaded. In a financialised age, such a mindset is hardly surprising. But it is misleading. You cannot digitise the spirit of a neighbourhood. You cannot outsource the making of community. Profit, extracted from a building you've never walked through in a town you've never cared for, risks becoming hollow—an abstraction without meaning.

This chapter invites you to pause, to rethink what it truly means to invest—and specifically, what it means to invest in property. It does not begin with amortisation schedules or yield calculations. It begins with the more enduring questions: What is wealth, to you? What sort of life do you wish to construct? What stories will your investments tell about you—both now and long after you are gone?

For unlike most other asset classes, property remembers.

More Than Bricks: Why Property Still Matters in a Digital Age

We live in an age of digital dominance. Cryptocurrencies, non-fungible tokens, algorithmic trading, and borderless capital flows have revolutionised the way we perceive value. The average investor can now trade global equities from a smartphone, build a portfolio without speaking to another human, and sell a position in seconds. This speed has its merits, but it also fosters a form of detachment. When everything is fluid, nothing feels permanent. When everything is abstract, nothing feels real.

Property resists this abstraction. It insists on presence. It forces you to confront geography, infrastructure, demographics, legislation, and community. It demands patience. It rewards attentiveness. And in return, it offers something rare: rootedness. In a world spinning faster by the day, that rootedness is not a liability—it is a competitive advantage.

Consider what happens during financial crises. When markets crash, digital wealth evaporates overnight. Derivatives implode. Tech valuations plummet. But properties, even if their paper value declines, do not disappear. A well-chosen home still offers shelter. A well-situated plot of land still holds future potential. Unlike intangible assets, property retains utility even in downturns. Its physicality makes it resilient.

Moreover, real estate operates on multiple dimensions. Yes, it can generate rental income and capital appreciation. But it can also function as a tool of autonomy: a hedge against inflation, a space for entrepreneurship, a vehicle for intergenerational wealth. It gives the owner not just profit, but power—the power to make decisions that affect others' lives and livelihoods. Ownership is never neutral.

And that is what sets property apart. It is more than a financial transaction. It is a political, emotional, and philosophical act. To own property is to shape the landscape around you—and, in turn, to be shaped by it.

The Investor's Inner Compass

Before you can build a property portfolio, you must build a point of view. That begins with understanding your internal compass: what drives your decisions, what shapes your tolerance for uncertainty, and what version of success you are actually chasing.

Many first-time investors never pause to ask these questions. They are swept into the current of conventional wisdom: buy low, sell high; leverage aggressively; seek "passive" income. But wisdom without context is dangerous. Strategy without self-awareness is reckless.

Are you investing to escape your job? To provide for a family? To make a mark? To retire early? Each motivation carries its own implications—for risk, for timing, for the kind of assets that make sense. A young, single professional with a mobile lifestyle will approach property very differently from a parent seeking stability in a particular school district. Neither is wrong. But neither should copy the other's playbook.

Moreover, your upbringing has likely influenced your view of money. Were you raised in a household that prized frugality? That feared debt? That viewed homeownership as a moral imperative—or a risky indulgence? These inherited beliefs, often subconscious, can affect how you respond to opportunity or threat. Until you name them, they will continue to steer you—often in invisible, unexamined ways.

This chapter helps you bring those beliefs to the surface. Because clarity is not a luxury in investing. It is a prerequisite. Before you choose a strategy, you must choose a stance: who you are, what you believe, and what kind of legacy you wish to construct.

Why Most First-Time Investors Get It Wrong

Real estate, as it is popularly portrayed, is rife with distortions. HGTV montages, glossy online listings, and overconfident social media influencers have created an unrealistic image of the first-time investor. In these narratives, properties are transformed in a weekend, tenants pay on time, and equity doubles within months. Risk is invisible, setbacks are brief, and success is inevitable.

The truth is less romantic. Real estate requires capital, time, emotional discipline, and often, a willingness to absorb discomfort. Leaky roofs. Late payments. Legal disputes. Deals that fall through. These are not anomalies—they are features of the landscape.

Where most beginners falter is not in effort, but in expectation. They overestimate what can be achieved in a year and underestimate what can be built over a decade. They conflate busyness with progress. They pursue passive income without realising that passivity is earned, not purchased.

This book does not promise ease. It promises insight. And insight begins with understanding what *not* to do—what assumptions to question, what shortcuts to resist, and which traps to avoid. There are patterns to failure in real estate, and many of them are preventable.

By examining those patterns up front, this chapter aims to give you a strategic edge—not just by revealing what's hard, but by showing you what's easier than you've been told. The goal is not to frighten, but to prepare. Because preparation breeds confidence—and confidence is the antidote to paralysis.

The Long Game: Thinking in Decades, Not Deals

Property rewards the patient. That may be the least fashionable truth in modern investing, but it is also the most enduring. Unlike tech stocks or crypto coins, a good property does not require dramatic intervention to yield results. What it requires is a willingness to think in decades—not deals.

That long-term lens changes everything. It alters how you evaluate locations, how you prioritise renovations, how you interact with tenants, and how you model returns. More importantly, it shifts your psychological framework. Instead of chasing quarterly gains, you begin to value compounding. Instead of obsessing over the next purchase, you start refining what you already own.

Delayed gratification is not a trait we are born with. It is a discipline we develop. In real estate, it is the difference between buying emotionally and buying intelligently. Between flipping a house and cultivating a portfolio. Between being a speculator and becoming a steward.

This chapter lays the foundation for that discipline. It introduces you to the rhythms of real estate—the slow build, the silent appreciation, the messy but manageable challenges that emerge over time. It urges you to think not in transactions, but in transitions. Not in hype cycles, but in horizons.

Because if wealth is to mean anything—if it is to be more than numbers or noise—it must be durable. It must reflect not just how much you earn, but how long it lasts, how well it serves, and what it enables you to do.

That kind of wealth doesn't just happen. It is built. One decision, one property, one strategy at a time.

And it begins by rethinking what you're really trying to achieve.

More Than Bricks: Why Property Still Matters in a Digital Age

There is something quietly radical about owning a piece of the physical world. In a time when so much of modern life has migrated to screens, clouds, and code, the act of acquiring land or a structure feels almost subversive. While markets cheer for speed and investors chase volatility, property persists—steady, unflashy, and deeply human. It doesn't ping, update, or disappear at the touch of a button. It simply stands, subject to weather, time, and care. And in that permanence lies its power.

To understand why real estate still matters—why it retains its primacy amid the seductive volatility of digital assets—we must begin with a simple truth: *physical space is non-substitutable.* You can't upload a house. You can't stream a parcel of land. And no matter how decentralised the next blockchain becomes, people will still need places to live, work, gather, and be. This makes property both a necessity and a reflection of our shared social contract. Unlike stocks, which are abstract slices of a corporation's future performance, or cryptocurrencies, which rely entirely on collective belief, property has intrinsic utility. It is shelter. It is infrastructure. It is memory.

In the financialised economy, value is increasingly divorced from tangible use. A single tweet can send a meme stock soaring; a venture fund can pour billions into a startup with no product, no customers, and no path to profitability. These dynamics reward narrative over fundamentals and often leave ordinary investors feeling unmoored—swept along by forces they neither trust nor fully understand. Property, by contrast, offers a kind of epistemological grounding. You can walk through it. You can point to its address. You can rent it, improve it, pass it on. That doesn't make it simple. But it makes it legible.

We are told to embrace agility, to prize liquidity, to keep everything "light." The dominant ethos is one of disembodiment—own nothing, rent everything, remain mobile. Yet humans are not weightless. We are physical beings with spatial needs, emotional ties, and community instincts. Property answers those needs in a way no portfolio ever could. It allows us to embed ourselves in a place, to steward something concrete, to accumulate meaning alongside equity. And meaning, increasingly, is the scarce asset.

This grounding function is particularly vital in periods of instability. During financial crises, technological disruptions, or pandemics, it becomes painfully clear which assets are luxuries and which are lifelines. In March 2020, as markets plunged and workplaces shuttered, it wasn't a stock ticker or NFT that provided security—it was the home. That flat with a balcony. That terrace with a garden. That family house with a locked door and a working boiler. Those who owned had options. Those who didn't, didn't.

To be clear, this is not a naïve celebration of bricks and mortar. Property comes with bureaucracy, complexity, and cost. It can be misused, speculated upon, hoarded, or turned into an instrument of exclusion. It can become just as abstract as a financial derivative when transformed into a trading vehicle for global capital. But properly understood—owned with intention, improved with care, and managed with foresight—real estate remains one of the few investments that can deliver multidimensional returns: financial, emotional, social, and generational.

Take, for example, a two-bedroom flat in East London purchased in 2010. At the time, the neighbourhood was in flux—post-industrial, diverse, not yet gentrified. The buyer, a mid-level architect, wasn't seeking a quick flip but a home with long-term potential. Over the next decade, as infrastructure improved and cultural investment flowed in, property values rose. But the real payoff wasn't just in appreciation. It was in stability. While rents around him soared, he paid a fixed mortgage. While neighbours moved frequently, he built local relationships. The property didn't just grow in value—it accrued memory. And now, as he contemplates letting the flat to tenants while relocating abroad, he is not merely a landlord. He is a custodian of place.

This is the overlooked story of property. Not the glamour of flipping, nor the fantasy of passive income with no labour, but the quiet accumulation of options—options that come from rootedness, not detachment. Property is slow capital. It compounds not just wealth, but identity.

Contrast this with the culture of hyper-velocity investing. Today's financial media promotes a kind of economic FOMO—fear of missing out on the next rally, the next token, the next market "event." Algorithms optimise for engagement, not wisdom. Advice is gamified. Research is commodified. And for those without a background in finance, the whole system begins to feel like a rigged game.

Against this backdrop, property offers clarity. Its risks are real, but not hidden. Its value drivers—location, condition, demand—are intelligible. And its timelines reward foresight, not frenzy. To invest in property is to resist the compulsion to act constantly. It is to adopt a rhythm more attuned to reality.

There is also a cultural dimension to consider. In many societies, property ownership is not just economic—it is existential. It represents arrival, stability, respectability. For immigrants, homeowners, parents, and elders, it often serves as the cornerstone of familial legacy. In the UK, the phrase "getting on the ladder" reflects this aspiration. Property is not just bought; it is built into identity.

But that cultural narrative, too, is changing. As prices rise and access narrows, younger generations are questioning whether property is still worth pursuing. Some dismiss it as an unattainable goal, others as a cumbersome burden. And yet, despite the barriers, the desire persists. Surveys across the UK, Canada, and Australia show that homeownership remains a top priority for millennials and Gen Z—not just for financial reasons, but for control, autonomy, and psychological security. Renting, however flexible, rarely offers those.

Even institutional investors—those with vast portfolios of liquid assets—are doubling down on property. Sovereign wealth funds, pension schemes, and private equity giants are buying commercial and residential assets at scale. Why? Because they understand what many individuals forget: that real estate provides not only returns, but ballast. It is the slow, sturdy counterweight to volatility elsewhere. And in a world where everything else is speeding up, ballast is not boring—it's essential.

Yet perhaps the most compelling case for property in a digital age is this: it cannot be replaced. Technologists may digitise transactions, virtualise tours, or tokenise ownership. But the asset itself—the physical space in a physical location—remains stubbornly real. It must be maintained. It must be managed. And its value will always reflect the intersecting forces of supply, demand, policy, and place.

None of this is to suggest that real estate is without risk. Markets crash. Tenants default. Roofs leak. Regulation shifts. And access, particularly in overheated cities, is a legitimate concern. But what distinguishes property from more speculative investments is its recoverability. Even a poor purchase may yield long-term gains if held and improved. Even a flat in a soft market still offers housing, utility, and dignity. The same cannot be said for digital assets that can become worthless overnight.

This is why thoughtful investors continue to gravitate toward property. Not because it is glamorous or effortless, but because it is real. It offers leverage, yes—but also leverage with responsibility. It demands attention. It teaches patience. And it rewards those who treat it not just as a transaction, but as a relationship.

The world will continue to digitise. New asset classes will emerge. Algorithms will grow more sophisticated. But people will still need places to live. Children will still need schools. Elders will still need care. Cities will still rise and fall according to where people want to be—and what they can afford to own. Amid all the noise, property remains the signal.

And for the investor willing to look past the hype, to engage with the complexity, and to build slowly but deliberately, that signal is worth hearing. Because at its best, real estate doesn't just preserve capital—it preserves possibility. It turns money into structure, structure into meaning, and meaning into memory.

That is not something you can download. And that is why property still matters.

The Investor's Inner Compass

Every investment decision is preceded by a decision about the self—conscious or not. Before numbers, before neighbourhoods, before financing structures or spreadsheets, there is a quieter set of variables that shapes everything: your motives, your fears, your beliefs about risk, control, time, and worth. Most new investors skip over this terrain, drawn into tactical questions—What should I buy? Where should I buy? How can I maximise yield?—without interrogating the personal frameworks that will ultimately determine their outcomes. But property investment, perhaps more than any other form of wealth-building, magnifies the investor's inner architecture. It exposes your temperament, your biases, your blind spots. If those foundations are unclear, even the most technically sound strategy is vulnerable.

Clarity, then, must precede strategy. Not as a philosophical exercise, but as a practical imperative. Without it, you're likely to chase the wrong deals, panic at the wrong times, or invest in properties that align with someone else's vision of success—not your own. The aim is not to find the "best" investment method in an abstract sense, but the one most consistent with who you are, what you value, and how you're willing to operate in the world.

Begin with the most basic question: *Why are you doing this?* It's easy to rattle off socially acceptable answers—financial freedom, passive income, early retirement—but those are outcomes, not drivers. Peel back another layer. Are you investing to escape something? To prove something? To compensate for a missed opportunity or childhood scarcity? Is it about control, security, legacy, or relevance? Your answer doesn't need to be noble. It needs to be honest. Because your motivations will shape every decision that follows—from the risk you tolerate, to the partners you choose, to the properties you favour.

Consider, for example, two investors with identical capital. One is driven by a desire for stability, scarred by economic uncertainty in their early life. The other is energised by growth, determined to scale quickly and create visible momentum. The first may gravitate towards modest, long-term rentals in reliable markets, even if the returns are slower. The second may pursue value-add opportunities, accept higher debt, and live with more volatility. Both strategies are valid. Neither is inherently better. But if either investor tried to mimic the other's playbook, they would likely fail—not because of the numbers, but because of the misalignment between strategy and self.

This is the essence of the investor's inner compass: understanding what kind of discomfort you are willing to bear. All investments come with discomfort—delays, doubts, setbacks, surprises. The trick is not to eliminate discomfort, but to choose the kind you can manage without breaking trust in yourself. For some, that means holding through a market dip. For others, it means stepping into negotiation rooms or managing difficult tenant dynamics. Risk, in this light, is not just a statistical measure—it's psychological. It's about how you respond when things go off-script.

Much of our response to risk is inherited. Not genetically, but culturally and experientially. Your early experiences with money—what was modelled, what was praised, what was punished—create a financial blueprint that persists into adulthood, often unconsciously. Were you raised in an environment where wealth was discussed openly, or avoided entirely? Was homeownership portrayed as a responsibility, a privilege, or a burden? Did your caregivers take risks, or avoid them at all costs? These questions are not rhetorical. They point to the stories you may be carrying into your investment thinking without realising it.

One common example is the myth of the "safe" property. Many first-time investors seek out a single-family home in a stable suburb, convinced it's a low-risk asset because it resembles what they grew up with. But familiarity is not the same as safety. What feels "safe" to one investor may in fact be risky—low yield, poor growth prospects, high maintenance—if not matched to the investor's financial goals and holding capacity. The emotional comfort of a particular asset class can blind investors to its actual performance.

Another inherited bias is the belief that debt is dangerous. This is not unfounded—debt can indeed be ruinous. But in property, strategic leverage is often the key to scaling sensibly. If you've been raised to see all debt as a moral failure or personal vulnerability, you may underutilise this tool or avoid deals that would otherwise serve your aims. The inverse is also true. Those raised in environments that glamorise leverage may become reckless, chasing overleveraged portfolios without the buffers to sustain shocks.

What matters is not which belief you start with, but whether you've examined it. Unexamined beliefs have a way of shaping portfolios in ways that look logical but are emotionally reactive. This is especially true in market downturns, when instinct can overrun analysis.

Investors with a clear internal compass can hold steady—or cut losses—based on principle, not panic.

Let's move from belief to temperament. Investment temperament is your behavioural response to uncertainty and control. Some people need high visibility and immediate feedback. Others thrive with ambiguity and delayed results. If you are the former, hands-on strategies—such as managing short-term rentals, overseeing renovations, or engaging directly with tenants—may suit you. You'll be able to see progress, make interventions, and feel actively involved. If you are the latter, a longer-term, less active strategy—such as acquiring and holding multifamily units with third-party management—may preserve your bandwidth and align better with your psychological profile.

There's a tendency among new investors to view temperament as something to conquer: to suppress fear, to master confidence, to adopt the mindset of someone they are not. This is misguided. The goal is not to become fearless. The goal is to become *aware*—to understand what triggers poor decisions and build around that. For instance, if you know you struggle with commitment, it may be smarter to start with a smaller property or a lower-stakes deal. If you tend to obsess over perfection, you may benefit from partnering with someone who has a bias for action.

Partnerships introduce a new layer of complexity. Your inner compass must be legible not just to you, but to anyone you invest with. Misaligned values between partners are a leading cause of property disputes and underperformance. If one partner views the property as a short-term wealth builder and the other sees it as a multi-generational asset, tension will arise—not just over outcomes, but over decisions at every stage. The earlier you clarify your own compass, the more effectively you can navigate these dynamics.

Clarity also impacts the kinds of markets you choose to enter. An investor seeking autonomy and resilience might favour smaller cities or regional towns, where entry costs are lower and cash flow steadier.

An investor focused on long-term appreciation may accept thinner margins today in exchange for stronger demographic trends tomorrow. But these choices only make sense when you know what you're optimising for. Are you trying to replace your income? Build generational wealth? Gain flexibility within ten years? Each objective carries different time horizons, risk profiles, and capital requirements. Without a clear orientation, you risk drifting—always busy, rarely aligned.

This is the danger of copying others. Property investment, unlike many forms of trading, is not a volume game. It is not about executing hundreds of micro-decisions quickly. It is about executing a smaller number of significant decisions wisely. This puts enormous pressure on those decisions to reflect your actual priorities—not someone else's strategy that happens to be trending.

Consider the case of a high-income professional in their late thirties, earning well but time-poor. They read about someone retiring early through aggressive house hacking, managing tenants in shared spaces, and flipping live-in projects. It sounds compelling—but it conflicts with their capacity, lifestyle, and risk tolerance. If they mimic that model, they may end up with burnout, poor execution, and strained finances. If they instead invest in fewer, better properties with reliable management, they may accept slower growth but sustain their effort—and peace of mind—for longer.

Legacy thinking is the final layer of the compass. Not everyone invests with the intention of passing assets down, but everyone invests with the intention of *impact*. Whether your goal is to retire earlier, provide for a child's education, support charitable work, or create optionality later in life, your investments reflect what you consider worthwhile. That reflection matters. Because over time, the properties you hold will not just accumulate capital—they will accumulate meaning. You will come to associate them with decisions, lessons, turning points. And when you look back, the question will not just be *what did this property earn?* but *what did it make possible?*

This is the deeper work of building an inner compass. It is not about finding a fixed identity or declaring yourself a particular "type" of investor. It is about cultivating self-awareness that is flexible but grounded—self-awareness that can adapt to changing markets without being whiplashed by them.

Strategy is important. Timing, leverage, location, yield—all of these matter. But they are only as effective as the clarity that directs them. Without a strong internal compass, even the best map will lead you astray. With it, even an imperfect plan can become a durable path.

Start there. Not with what to buy, but with who you are when you buy it. That, more than any market trend or expert forecast, will shape the investor you become—and the legacy you leave behind.

Why Most First-Time Investors Get It Wrong

The most dangerous misconception in property investing isn't about interest rates, market timing, or even location. It's the belief that success is inevitable—that with a little enthusiasm, a few YouTube tutorials, and a willingness to "get on the ladder," everything else will fall into place. This idea is not just misleading—it's costly. For first-time investors, the real risk rarely lies in catastrophic failure. It lies in slow erosion: the property that underperforms for a decade, the financing that drains liquidity, the partnership that sours quietly, the plan that never quite aligns with the investor's actual life. These missteps often begin with a seductive but false narrative: that property is a simple, passive, and foolproof path to wealth.

Part of the problem is cultural. Property investment has been flattened into a storyline: the makeover montage, the tidy flip, the polished photo of keys handed over. Television programmes, social media, and influencer-led courses have turned the process into spectacle—where complexity is edited out and the emotional highs are curated for maximum appeal. Shows like *Homes Under the Hammer*, *Property Brothers*, and their international clones imply that anyone with a sledgehammer and a spreadsheet can convert bricks into capital. What they rarely show are the holding costs, the council delays, the sleepless nights spent calculating whether a boiler replacement will derail cash flow for six months. The result is a skewed set of expectations: underestimating what's hard, overestimating what's easy, and mistaking effort for expertise.

One of the most persistent myths is the allure of "passive income." It's a phrase so overused it has lost meaning—sold as the dream outcome of property ownership, where money flows while you sleep and wealth compounds without work. While real estate can indeed produce recurring income, there is nothing passive about acquiring, managing, and maintaining physical assets. Even with professional management, the owner remains responsible—for decision-making, oversight, and risk. Vacancy, repairs, tenant disputes, tax filings, insurance adjustments—these are not minor footnotes. They are part of the business. And in property, you are always in the business.

New investors are often caught off guard by the sheer administrative drag of ownership. A missed document, a misclassified expense, or a delayed inspection can unravel a project or trigger cascading costs. And because the industry operates on long cycles—monthly rental income, annual tax returns, multi-year appreciation—mistakes compound slowly but stubbornly. Unlike day trading or startup investing, where feedback is fast and brutal, property punishes carelessness with silence. A poorly chosen property may not collapse, but it will quietly underperform, siphoning time, energy, and returns until the investor gives up or sells at a loss.

Financing is another minefield where first-timers routinely falter. The obsession with securing "the lowest rate" distracts from a more crucial question: *what is the structure of the debt, and does it match the strategy?* A cheap loan on an illiquid asset with short-term repayment terms is a trap, not a bargain. Similarly, investors often fail to budget adequately for initial costs—legal fees, survey reports, stamp duty, furnishings, vacancy periods. These are not incidental. They can represent 5–10% of total investment capital, and if not properly forecast, they can deplete emergency reserves before the first tenant ever moves in.

Risk tolerance is misunderstood, too. Many first-time investors believe that buying a physical asset feels "safer" than equities or crypto. This perception leads them to overlook genuine exposure—such as geographic concentration, leverage risk, liquidity constraints, or regulatory shifts. A buy-to-let in a single-industry town with falling population may look attractive on paper, but it's functionally as risky as a volatile stock—just harder to exit. Without rigorous due diligence, property can feel safe but behave dangerously.

Expectations around cash flow often compound the problem. Beginners are routinely advised to chase properties that "cash flow from day one"—a well-intentioned idea that's frequently misapplied. Too often, investors compromise on asset quality, tenant pool, or location just to secure a few hundred pounds of net monthly income. What's missed is that early cash flow is only valuable if it's durable—supported by tenant demand, economic stability, and responsible maintenance. A property that cash flows today but deteriorates structurally or socially over the next five years can become a liability faster than a spreadsheet can warn you.

Perhaps most counterintuitive is the idea that the hardest part of property investing is not the acquisition—it's the stewardship. Buying is episodic. Ownership is continuous. It's what happens after the deal closes that defines the investment: how the property is cared for, how relationships are managed, how capital improvements are timed, how exit strategies are evaluated. Most first-time investors are psychologically geared up for the chase and the purchase. They are not prepared for the ongoing responsibilities—strategic, financial, and emotional—that come with being an owner. It is this mismatch that leads to burnout, disillusionment, and the eventual selling off of assets at suboptimal terms.

This is also why many new investors skip essential learning stages. They may bypass property management basics, delegate too early, or attempt to scale before their first property has even stabilised. In some cases, they are pushed to expand rapidly by online communities or mentors who champion "going big" over getting smart. The emphasis on scale becomes a badge of honour, even when the investor lacks systems, discipline, or experience. And like any overleveraged ambition, it works—until it doesn't.

But not all is doom. There are aspects of property investing that are easier than many newcomers assume—if approached correctly. Building basic competence in valuation, negotiation, and financial analysis does not require a finance degree. With disciplined study, clear mentors, and grounded expectations, these skills are accessible. Likewise, not every deal requires vast capital. Creative entry points—joint ventures, lease options, fractional investments—can lower the barrier. The key is to pursue simplicity with sophistication: to understand the instruments fully before employing them, and to know where you are most likely to make unforced errors.

It is also easier than many believe to find good tenants—if the property is well-maintained, priced appropriately, and situated in a market with stable demand. Most horror stories about tenant behaviour stem from poor screening, weak contracts, or desperate pricing strategies. Good property management is not about luck. It's about systems. Learning to assess character, enforce boundaries, and manage expectations is as much a people skill as a technical one.

What's often overlooked is that the most successful investors are not necessarily the most aggressive or even the most knowledgeable. They are the most *clear-minded*. They understand their own biases. They pace themselves. They approach each property not as a shortcut to wealth, but as a micro-business—something that requires thought, care, adaptation, and integrity. This is the mindset that prevents major missteps. Not because the investor never errs, but because they learn to err in manageable ways.

Ultimately, most first-time investors get it wrong not because they are unmotivated or uninformed, but because they are misaligned—misaligned with their expectations, their risk profile, their capital, their bandwidth. They want a part-time outcome from a part-time effort, without recognising that property rewards the long view. It tests character as much as strategy. And that test is not a one-off—it's cumulative.

Getting it right, then, is less about avoiding every mistake and more about developing resilience. A first deal that underwhelms can still be the start of a strong portfolio if the investor is willing to reflect, recalibrate, and recommit. But that requires a mindset shift—from the fantasy of passive riches to the discipline of active learning. From mimicry to mastery. From speed to staying power.

The best advice for any first-time investor is not what to buy or where to buy. It is to slow down long enough to understand the terrain—external and internal. To invest not just money, but attention. Because in real estate, as in life, the early moves cast long shadows. And those who begin with clarity, humility, and focus are not only more likely to build wealth—they are more likely to keep it.

The Long Game: Thinking in Decades, Not Deals

The greatest returns in real estate rarely come from brilliant purchases. They come from holding on. Through cycles. Through uncertainty. Through boredom. The real skill in property investing is not spotting a deal—it's staying the course long enough for value to mature. In a culture that rewards instant gratification, fast exits, and short-term optics, thinking in decades has become a radical act. But it is also the core discipline that separates speculative flurries from enduring wealth.

Modern finance, shaped by quarterly earnings and real-time trading, has conditioned us to think in flashes—events, spikes, exits. Patience, once considered a virtue, now reads as hesitation. Delayed gratification sounds like poor branding. Yet property, by its nature, is an asset class built on the slow accumulation of value. It resists haste. It rewards consistency. And it requires investors to align their timelines not with quarterly charts but with generational outcomes.

This distinction is not abstract. Consider the difference between a buyer who flips properties every 12–18 months and one who acquires and holds well-positioned rentals for 20 years. The former may earn visible profits quickly, perhaps even impressive ones. But their returns are punctuated by friction: transaction costs, taxes, renovation overruns, and the psychological strain of constantly seeking the next opportunity. The latter, by contrast, may see slower appreciation in the early years—but benefits from compounding rent increases, mortgage amortisation, and inflation-protected value growth. They are not hustling for the next win; they are stewarding a growing base of productive assets. Over time, the quiet investor often outpaces the active one—not just financially, but in bandwidth, resilience, and optionality.

Understanding this dynamic begins with reframing what wealth means. True wealth is not just a number. It is control over time, decisions, and quality of life. It is the ability to wait—because you do not need to act under pressure. That ability is precisely what long-term property investing cultivates. A mortgage paid down over 25 years is not glamorous, but it is powerful. It creates equity without fanfare. It builds freedom slowly, almost invisibly. And yet many investors undervalue this process because it lacks spectacle.

Behavioural economists call this bias "present bias"—the tendency to prioritise immediate rewards over larger, delayed ones. Numerous studies, from the famous Stanford marshmallow experiment to recent work in behavioural finance, demonstrate how consistently humans undervalue the future. This is particularly acute in investing.

The psychological itch to act, to optimise, to be seen to be doing something, leads many investors to sell prematurely or reshuffle their portfolios unnecessarily. In property, this often takes the form of flipping or trading up too early—cashing out on modest gains instead of allowing compound growth to take root.

But the most successful investors are often those who resist the urge to intervene unnecessarily. They buy quality assets—well-located, structurally sound, with solid demand fundamentals—and then allow time to do its work. This doesn't mean neglect. It means resisting overreaction. It means having the discipline to improve a property strategically without falling into the trap of over-capitalising. It means knowing when to refinance and when to stay put. Most of all, it means learning to think in years, not quarters.

One London-based investor, for example, acquired a semi-detached house in Walthamstow in 2005, when the area was still considered transitional. The property was modest, the initial yield acceptable but unremarkable. Over the years, as infrastructure improved, the community matured, and demand steadily increased, the property tripled in value. But the real payoff wasn't just the capital appreciation. It was the consistency of rental income, the low tenant turnover, and the ability to leverage the equity into a second purchase. There were no flashy moves, no viral social media stories. Just patient stewardship and long-term orientation. And the outcome? Financial independence by 50—not through innovation, but through endurance.

It's important to recognise that long-term thinking is not simply about holding property indefinitely. It's about building frameworks that respect time. That might mean buying with a 20-year horizon but re-evaluating every five. It might mean choosing properties that allow for phased improvements, rather than maxing out value upfront. It might mean planning for intergenerational transfer, or integrating properties into broader financial plans. The point is not to cling to assets for sentimentality. It's to make decisions that reflect long arcs, not reactive pulses.

This approach also buffers against market cycles. Property markets, like all markets, are cyclical. Prices rise, stagnate, correct, and rise again. Investors who think in decades are less vulnerable to downturns—not because they avoid loss, but because they can ride it out. Time is the ultimate risk mitigator. It absorbs volatility. It smooths out timing errors. It allows rents to catch up, debts to decline, and value to recover. Short-term investors often panic when markets correct. Long-term investors see corrections as normal. Sometimes even as opportunities.

But long-term thinking requires a certain temperament. It demands low ego, high discipline, and a tolerance for deferred recognition. You must be comfortable not "winning" in visible ways—at least not quickly. You must learn to prioritise sustainability over excitement. Many investors struggle with this, especially early on. The temptation to accelerate, to impress, to compare against faster peers, can be intense. The solution is not to suppress ambition. It is to rechannel it—towards depth, quality, and compounding results.

There is also an ethical dimension to long-termism in property. Investors who think in decades are more likely to maintain assets responsibly, treat tenants with respect, and contribute positively to neighbourhoods. They are not extracting value—they are participating in its cultivation. This mindset fosters better outcomes not only for the investor, but for the broader community. It aligns financial interest with civic impact. And while it may not produce the fastest gains, it often produces the most meaningful ones.

Thinking long-term doesn't mean ignoring the present. It means using the present to build leverage for the future. This can take many forms: paying down principal early, reinvesting rental profits into improvements, building relationships with local tradespeople, or studying zoning changes that may affect future development potential. These actions may seem minor now. Over 10 or 20 years, they compound into major advantages—reduced costs, stronger networks, expanded opportunities.

Strategic patience is not the same as passivity. It is a deliberate choice to act at the right tempo—not faster than necessary, not slower than prudent. And it's worth noting that long-term decisions often feel boring. They don't deliver dopamine hits. They don't yield headlines. But they work. Quietly. Repeatedly. Predictably.

This is not to romanticise the long view. There are times when exiting early is wise. There are markets where long holds become burdens. The point is not to adopt a rigid doctrine, but to use time as a tool. To understand that the most powerful lever in real estate is often the least dramatic one: holding well. Not forever. But well.

Too many first-time investors focus on deal velocity—how many, how fast, how big. The more profound question is: *what can you hold onto long enough to matter?* Because it's not your entry that defines your wealth. It's your capacity to stay invested with clarity, integrity, and foresight. That's the long game. And it's where real wealth begins.

Chapter 2
Starting Small, Smart, and Strategic

The mythology of real estate is often told in oversized terms—skyscrapers rising from bare earth, portfolios sprawling across postcodes, renovations spun into television-worthy profit. Success is tallied in square footage, net yield, equity multiples. Yet, for those stepping into the field for the first time, the story almost never begins that way. It starts, more often than not, in cramped rooms, imperfect choices, and unglamorous beginnings. And that is precisely as it should be. The value of starting small is not merely about hedging risk. It lies in cultivating instincts no compound-interest chart will ever reveal: discernment, perspective, pattern recognition. Property is one of the rare asset classes where modest openings can yield disproportionate returns—not necessarily financial at first, but strategic. This chapter is concerned with how to make those small openings matter.

To begin small is not to concede defeat. It is a principle. One well-executed deal, however minor on paper, can grant access to capital, credibility, and networks that shift what is possible in later moves. The popular imagination frames real estate as a drama of bold leaps; the truth is closer to architecture. Foundations laid carefully, brick by brick. The misaligned brick, placed in haste, cracks everything that comes after.

Small, however, is not synonymous with trivial. Quite the opposite. The so-called micro move—purchasing a modest flat with two friends, securing a lease-option on a tired property in a transitional district, or simply letting out a spare room—becomes an education in itself. Contracts, maintenance, tenants, financing, emotions—each makes itself known. Spreadsheets may model returns, but they cannot prepare you for the knot in your stomach during a tenant dispute, or the grit required when a boiler fails midwinter. These beginnings shape not just what you own, but how you carry yourself as an investor.

One of the more persistent myths is that momentum requires money. Not so. It requires motion, and motion demands leverage—

financial, intellectual, social, or temporal. Without capital, you can lean on trust. Without knowledge, on hustle. The important thing is to begin where you are, not where the textbooks insist you must arrive before qualifying. Saving £50,000, waiting for the "perfect" market, memorising every financing model—often these are forms of procrastination disguised as prudence. At some point, inertia must be broken.

That said, reckless action is as dangerous as endless delay. A deliberate frame of strategy must sit alongside small beginnings. Co-investing, for instance, can multiply opportunity—if roles, risks, and exit routes are defined before the ink is dry on a contract. Poorly structured, it strains both wallets and friendships. Done carefully, it creates momentum far greater than any individual could achieve.

Equally, alternative routes deserve recognition. Traditional ownership—deposit, mortgage, title—is not the only key in the ring. Lease options, rent-to-own agreements, fractional platforms, even REITs, open other doors. House hacking, now almost folklore among younger investors, remains one of the shrewdest approaches: live in one part of a property, let out the other, and learn the rhythms of tenants, cash flow, and repair in real time—without the barrier of a six-figure deposit.

And then there are the places others overlook. Neighbourhoods just beyond the commuter line, districts awaiting new transit links, corners of towns carrying outdated reputations—all can harbour disproportionate potential. These are not headline "hotspots"; they are the slow burns, the margins where price and possibility diverge most. To begin small in such spaces is not guaranteed triumph, but it is often where the boldest asymmetry lies.

Still, the greatest return from a first deal is rarely financial. It is educational. Too many treat their inaugural property as a trophy—something to parade, validate, or accelerate towards a career. But the truer role of that first step is pedagogical. It reveals your blind spots, stresses your systems, unmasks your defaults under pressure. The profits may be modest, perhaps even losses. That is not failure. That is tuition.

Hence why property should not be mistaken for a game. The goal is not to "win," but to build. These early experiments shape investor intelligence—not only knowledge, but wisdom. When to walk away, how to price uncertainty, when to heed intuition, how to recover from missteps—none of this appears in the neat tables of a calculator, yet all of it determines your long-term path.

Consider, for example, three young friends in Manchester, pooling £12,000 each for a terraced house in a ward slowly stirring from industrial decline. The renovation went over budget. The yield was respectable but not remarkable. And yet, the lessons were invaluable: planning permissions, trade quotes, lease negotiations, partner dynamics. Within three years, they refinanced, moved to a second property, and each took their own trajectory—one into conversions, another into passive investing, the third into development. The first house was no jackpot. It was a hinge.

The question at this stage is not how much you acquire, but what structure you build. Are you learning frameworks, or merely imitating someone else's criteria? Are you anchoring confidence in cash flow and capital growth, or in the thrill of ownership itself? These small distinctions define an investment identity—and once set, it is not easily undone. Begin with impatience, and impatience becomes habit. Begin with humility and intention, and you will cultivate a practice that compounds.

Starting small, then, is not about thinking small. It is about respecting order. Leverage must be earned, not assumed. Partnerships demand clarity as well as contracts. Misunderstood markets are not dead ends but frontiers, if read correctly. Creative structures are not gimmicks but valid tools, provided they are grasped deeply. Above all, the first property is not a legacy. It is a laboratory.

This chapter pushes back against the belief that success must be immediate or impressive. It offers strategies that value depth over display, process over performance. It equips you to find your edge, wherever you start. Because in real estate, the foundation matters more than the façade. And the most reliable way to build that foundation is to begin as small as possible—deliberately, intelligently, with an eye not just to profit, but to the kind of investor you are becoming.

Micro Moves with Macro Impact

In property investment, as in most fields of enduring value creation, the most powerful actions are often the least theatrical. Media narratives tend to focus on dramatic acquisitions, celebrity investors, or high-stakes development projects, implying that meaningful success requires exceptional capital or insider access. But for first-time investors, this is both misleading and counterproductive. The truth is that well-timed, well-structured micro moves—small, deliberate steps taken with strategic intent—can initiate a compounding sequence of financial and experiential leverage. And they often outperform larger, riskier ventures when measured in terms of return on learning, optionality, and long-term positioning.

The myth of the "big break" is a persistent one. Many novice investors imagine that their first move needs to be transformational—a three-bed rental in a rising market, a buy-renovate-refinance project with high yield potential, or a multi-unit block offering immediate cash flow. In reality, these larger plays often demand an operational maturity, financial buffer, and mental bandwidth that new investors have not yet developed. What's more, they introduce a level of downside risk that's inappropriate for the early stages of a property career. The smarter path is often less ambitious in scope but more sophisticated in structure: a micro move that generates momentum without overwhelming your resources or distorting your learning curve.

Micro doesn't mean random or trivial. It means calibrated. A £15,000 investment into a fractional ownership platform with strong governance can serve as a low-friction introduction to capital allocation, market behaviour, and legal structure. A co-investment with two friends into a modest buy-to-let in a secondary city may yield limited income at first, but provides valuable exposure to the interpersonal dynamics, cash management, and maintenance rhythms that define real estate management in practice. These kinds of projects offer controlled exposure to complexity without catastrophic risk—training the investor in the habits of discernment, not just ambition.

Consider a case from Glasgow: two junior architects, both earning under £35,000 annually, pooled £10,000 each and partnered with a third friend in IT, who contributed legal and tech support in lieu of capital. Together, they purchased a repossessed one-bedroom flat in a transitional neighbourhood for £65,000. The renovation was modest—cosmetic fixes, compliance upgrades, and furnishings. The rental income wasn't life-changing. But the structure of the partnership, the clarity of roles, and the discipline of shared accountability gave them something rare: a low-cost, high-yield apprenticeship in real estate execution. Within two years, they refinanced, extracted equity, and applied it toward a second, slightly larger property—this time with stronger yields and a more refined operational model. What began as a micro move became a strategic flywheel.

This kind of early success is not formulaic, but it is repeatable. It starts with one core principle: *investing at your edge*. That is, operating where your skills, capital, and risk tolerance are fully engaged—but not overstretched. This differs radically from investing at your limit, which often leads to errors, stress, and capital depletion. A micro move respects your edge. It challenges you without destabilising you. It allows you to learn while staying solvent, to move forward while remaining composed.

One of the most effective ways to execute micro moves is through co-investment. This doesn't mean partnering for the sake of splitting the bill. It means structuring partnerships where each party brings distinct value—whether capital, expertise, time, or networks—and where the combined effort creates an outcome none could achieve alone. This form of leverage is more resilient than debt and more flexible than equity. But it only works when expectations are not only discussed but formalised—through contracts, exit clauses, capital call agreements, and aligned incentives. Too many informal partnerships disintegrate over ambiguity. Micro does not mean casual. In fact, the smaller the deal, the more vital it is that roles and terms are professionally defined.

Buying into overlooked neighbourhoods is another high-leverage micro strategy. Markets that are still forming, often characterised by mixed reputations, slow gentrification, or underpriced infrastructure, offer asymmetric upside for early entrants who are willing to do the work of discovery. This does not mean chasing the next Shoreditch or Digbeth. It means studying planning applications, transport links, demographic shifts, and public investment trends to identify areas where the fundamentals are improving before the narrative catches up. The key is not prediction, but positioning. A modest flat in an area gaining its first co-working hub or community café may perform better over ten years than a premium property in a saturated central postcode. But this requires a long-view mindset, not a yield-obsessed one.

One recurring mistake new investors make is dismissing small deals as "not worth it." This thinking is often inherited from institutional finance, where economies of scale are essential. But individual investors play by different rules. For them, *access precedes scale.* The goal is not to win big early—it is to get in, get oriented, and get smarter. A micro move provides that access. It teaches timing, sourcing, negotiation, legal process, and emotional control—all in a live environment with real stakes. These are skills that cannot be learned in theory. And once learned, they compound.

Micro moves also offer psychological advantages. They minimise the fear of failure by keeping the stakes manageable. They build credibility without requiring overstatement. And they allow for agile experimentation. If the first strategy doesn't work—say, short-term letting underperforms—you can pivot without catastrophic loss. This feedback loop builds resilience. And resilience is the most underrated trait in successful investors. Not boldness. Not brilliance. But the ability to stay in the game long enough for probability to tilt in your favour.

There's also a powerful ethical component. Investors who begin with modest, community-oriented projects—rather than extractive, high-yield plays—are more likely to see their role as stewards, not speculators. This shift in mindset leads to better tenant relationships, more thoughtful renovations, and more sustainable growth. It embeds the investor in the fabric of a neighbourhood rather than isolating them from it. That relational capital, though harder to quantify, often proves decisive when scaling up: securing off-market deals, sourcing trusted contractors, or navigating planning discussions with local authorities.

This strategic humility—starting small with depth, not bravado—also produces a rare kind of clarity. You learn where you genuinely have edge and where you don't. You discover your actual appetite for risk, your comfort with ambiguity, and your tolerance for operational complexity. These are insights that will shape every future deal. And they are rarely available to those who try to start big, fast, or flashy.

Perhaps the most underappreciated impact of micro moves is their ability to unlock compounding trust. When you complete one small project well—on time, on budget, with integrity—you create proof. Proof that you are reliable. That you deliver. That you understand the process. That trust is a form of currency. It draws in collaborators, capital, and counsel. It accelerates everything that follows. And it's usually earned not in high-stakes situations but in small, consistent, competently executed transactions.

In a market culture that prizes scale, sophistication, and spectacle, the investor willing to start small—but start smart—gains an unspoken advantage. They are not performing. They are practising. They are not chasing returns—they are compounding capability. And over time, that capability becomes its own form of leverage—

more durable than money, more adaptable than metrics, and more predictive of sustained success than any early headline yield.

If you're starting out in property, the most important question is not *how big can I go?* but *how well can I begin?* Because the small moves, done strategically, don't just get you on the ladder. They shape how you climb it. And in a game where staying power matters more than speed, that difference is decisive.

Partnerships Without Regret

There is a particular kind of optimism that surrounds the idea of investing in property with people you already trust—family members, long-time friends, business associates. It feels efficient, intuitive, even natural. You pool resources, divide responsibilities, and move faster than you could alone. Yet, for all the emotional and strategic appeal, the track record of informal property partnerships is mixed at best. When they work, they can fast-track growth and deepen mutual success. When they fail, they leave financial damage, emotional fallout, and legal entanglements that can last years. The difference rarely lies in the asset—it lies in the structure. The most enduring partnerships are not built on goodwill alone, but on clarity, contractual rigour, and aligned expectations.

The mistake most first-time partners make is conflating relational trust with transactional understanding. Knowing someone well does not equate to understanding how they behave under financial stress, operational strain, or shifting market conditions. You may trust a sibling with your life, but that doesn't mean you share a common definition of risk, a compatible work ethic, or an identical view on how profits should be split. Property investment amplifies these differences, especially when real money, tenants, maintenance issues, or exit decisions are involved. What felt like a shared vision at the outset can quickly fracture when tested by delayed renovations, rising interest rates, or diverging life plans.

Partnerships succeed when they are designed to *contain friction, not rely on the absence of it.* This means building mechanisms into the agreement that anticipate disagreement. Who decides when to sell? What happens if one partner wants out early? How are additional capital injections handled? What if someone misses a mortgage payment? These are not cynical questions—they are structural ones. Just as a well-built house is designed to withstand wind and moisture, a well-built partnership is designed to withstand pressure without collapse.

One particularly instructive example comes from a group of cousins in Birmingham who co-invested in a two-up-two-down terrace property, intending to renovate and let it out to students. They were close, grew up together, and shared an enthusiasm for property. But within six months, tension emerged. One cousin moved abroad unexpectedly, another faced job instability, and the third—now responsible for management—felt overburdened and undercompensated. There was no written agreement, no defined exit plan, and no clarity on who controlled the bank account. The project stalled. The property sat empty. The relationship frayed. Eventually, it was sold at a loss—financially modest, but emotionally costly. The failure wasn't due to malice or laziness. It was due to ambiguity.

Contrast this with a smaller partnership between two unrelated colleagues in Bristol, who bought a compact flat near a hospital with the intention of letting it to healthcare workers. From the outset, they engaged a solicitor to draft a partnership agreement that addressed equity shares, expense contributions, decision rights, and dispute resolution mechanisms. They met monthly, documented decisions, and kept communication professional. When one partner later decided to use their equity to purchase a home, the process of buying out their share had already been agreed upon. The partnership concluded cleanly, with both parties satisfied. The difference wasn't scale—it was design.

Formal structure does not kill trust; it preserves it. A well-drafted agreement acts not as a sign of distrust, but as a recognition that trust is too valuable to leave unprotected. It clarifies roles, reduces assumptions, and provides a neutral reference point when emotions rise. For this reason, *every* property partnership—regardless of relationship closeness—should begin with a written agreement prepared by a qualified solicitor. This should cover not only capital contributions and ownership shares, but management responsibilities, income distributions, exit protocols, and dispute resolution methods.

Another critical element is alignment on investment philosophy. It's not enough to agree on the property itself. Partners must agree on why they are investing, what success looks like, and how much uncertainty they're willing to tolerate. One partner may see the investment as a long-term hold; another may want to exit within five years. One may prioritise yield; another capital growth. One may favour reinvestment of profits; another may want to withdraw income annually. If these philosophical orientations diverge, the strategy will drift—or worse, split.

The operational side also needs thoughtful delegation. Many partnerships collapse under the weight of unclear or unequal responsibilities. Who handles tenant communication? Who manages repairs, insurance renewals, annual filings? It's tempting to assume things will balance out naturally, but they rarely do. Without explicit task assignment—and agreed-upon compensation for those tasks—resentment builds. One partner ends up doing more, the other feeling marginalised. Preventing this requires more than a checklist. It requires a conversation about capacity, strengths, and fairness. Not every partner needs to contribute equally, but every contribution must be agreed and valued.

Capital structures need similar clarity. If one partner contributes more equity, how is that rewarded—via ownership percentage, interest on capital, or preferred returns? What happens if the property needs additional capital later—does everyone contribute proportionally? Can someone decline, and if so, what are the consequences? These issues often emerge not during acquisition, but during challenge—when a boiler breaks, a tenant leaves, or a remortgage is delayed. Agreements made under calm conditions are what enable calm decisions when conditions change.

It's also wise to structure partnerships with built-in flexibility. Life circumstances evolve. Someone moves. Someone changes career. Someone gets married, divorced, or has children. A well-constructed agreement should allow partners to buy each other out, bring in new partners, or exit gracefully—without triggering conflict or needing a court. This is particularly vital in family partnerships, where personal and financial entanglements can become generational if not handled carefully.

There are also tax considerations. Joint ownership can have different implications depending on how it is structured—tenants in common vs joint tenants, partnership vs limited company, individual vs shared tax bands. Choosing the right structure should be driven not by what's popular, but by your specific circumstances—income levels, future plans, and national regulations. Seeking proper tax advice before entering a partnership is not optional. It's foundational.

Beyond structure, the emotional dimension must be acknowledged. Partnerships involve more than property—they involve identity, pride, ego, and occasionally fear. Disagreements are not just about money—they're about feeling heard, respected, and in control. Successful partners learn how to separate emotion from decision. They commit to regular communication, treat each other with professional respect, and understand that disagreement is not a threat but a necessity. When two or more people work together in any meaningful venture, tension is a sign that important things are being negotiated—not a sign of dysfunction.

Perhaps the greatest advantage of a well-formed property partnership is the multiplier effect. One person can do a lot. Two aligned people, with complementary skills, can do exponentially more. They can pursue bigger deals, access better financing, and bring diverse perspectives to complex decisions. But this advantage only manifests when the foundation is sound. Without it, the same partnership becomes a liability—a source of friction rather than force.

The best partnerships are not built on enthusiasm or proximity. They are built on clarity. Clarity about the purpose of the partnership. Clarity about each person's role and value. Clarity about the rules that govern the enterprise. With that clarity, partnerships can accelerate your path to sustainable property success. Without it, they can derail even the most promising efforts.

The goal is not to avoid partnering. It is to partner well. Thoughtfully. Deliberately. With structure that serves both the relationship and the deal. Because in property—as in any enduring enterprise—the most valuable equity is not just financial. It's relational. And protecting that requires more than trust. It requires terms.

Creative Entry Points

There is a quiet but pervasive misconception that real estate investment belongs exclusively to those who already own property, earn six-figure salaries, or have inherited capital. The image of the investor—still prevalent in media and marketing—tends to be polished and established: someone who already has the keys, not someone reaching for them. This illusion is reinforced by gatekeeping narratives around deposit requirements, mortgage pre-approvals, and the pressure to "buy right" from the outset. What these narratives miss—or obscure entirely—is that access to property does not have to begin with ownership in the conventional sense. It can begin with access to *function*, *cash flow*, and *strategic position.* The most resourceful investors don't wait to "look" like investors.

They find creative points of entry that match their reality while setting the stage for future expansion.

These unconventional approaches aren't just for those with limited capital. They are increasingly used by experienced investors seeking flexibility, lower risk, or niche exposure. But they're especially powerful for first-timers who are asset-light but mindset-rich—those with hustle, clarity, and a willingness to step sideways into an industry that often presents itself as vertical. Creative entry points aren't about cutting corners. They're about adjusting the route without diluting the rigour.

One of the most accessible and misunderstood strategies is house hacking. The term, popularised in North America but increasingly relevant in UK and European markets, refers to any living arrangement where the investor simultaneously occupies and monetises the property. This might mean renting out a spare bedroom, converting a garage into a studio, or purchasing a small multi-unit building and residing in one unit while letting the others. The appeal lies in the dual benefit: reduced personal housing costs and hands-on landlord experience. What makes house hacking potent is not just its economics—it's the educational return. The investor is immersed in the daily realities of property management: rent collection, repair coordination, tenant relations. These lessons are absorbed at close range, and often under financial pressure. That intimacy with the process produces sharper, more grounded future decisions.

In urban markets where prices are high and multi-unit properties scarce, house hacking can take more creative forms. A junior doctor in London, for instance, rented a two-bedroom flat near her hospital and sublet the second bedroom on a rolling six-month agreement, offsetting over 60% of her rent. While technically not an owner, she used this arrangement to build savings, learn informal tenant management, and eventually transition into ownership with far greater confidence. The strategy was low-capital, high-learning. And for her, it was the bridge between ambition and access.

Another compelling path is lease options—a structure often ignored by traditional buyers but regularly employed by sophisticated investors. A lease option grants the right (but not the obligation) to purchase a property at an agreed price within a specified timeframe, typically in exchange for an upfront fee and monthly rent. The investor gains control over the asset without needing to secure a mortgage immediately. For sellers, particularly those with vacant properties, financial distress, or slow-moving listings, lease options can provide cash flow and eventual exit. For buyers, they offer a chance to test the asset, improve its value, or wait for financing to mature. This model requires deep due diligence, strong legal support, and excellent negotiation skills—but it has the potential to unlock deals that traditional financing would exclude.

Critics of lease options often point to complexity and regulatory grey areas, and rightly so—there are predatory versions of these agreements that exploit unsophisticated sellers. But when structured ethically and transparently, lease options can produce genuine win-win outcomes. An investor in the Midlands negotiated a lease option on a three-bed house in a slowly appreciating neighbourhood, paying £500 per month for three years with the option to buy at a pre-agreed price. During the term, they improved the property, built a tenant track record, and secured a mortgage using the income history. When they exercised the option, the property had appreciated by over 15%, and they acquired it with both equity and experience in hand.

Fractional ownership is another path reshaping what access to property can mean. Platforms now exist that allow investors to purchase equity stakes in residential or commercial properties, often starting from as little as £1,000. These models vary—some are structured as equity partnerships, others as debt instruments, and still others as hybrid models with income-sharing features. The key advantage is diversification. Rather than betting heavily on a single asset, investors can spread exposure across multiple markets, property types, and risk profiles. This is particularly attractive for professionals with strong income but limited time or desire for hands-on management.

Sceptics question whether fractional ownership is "real" property investment. After all, you can't visit the asset, change its layout, or evict a tenant. But this critique misunderstands the core function of real estate in a portfolio. For many investors, the goal is not control—it's exposure. They want income, appreciation, and inflation hedging. Fractional models, when properly regulated and transparently operated, deliver these outcomes without the operational burden. And for new investors, they offer a way to begin compounding capital while observing the behaviours of property markets in real time.

Real Estate Investment Trusts (REITs) also fall into this category. These publicly traded vehicles allow individuals to invest in professionally managed portfolios of income-producing real estate. Unlike fractional platforms, REITs offer immediate liquidity, transparency, and regulatory oversight. They also typically provide dividend income, making them a useful bridge between equities and direct property ownership. While REITs lack the tangibility and leverage potential of physical property, they are an underutilised training ground. Investors who study REIT performance, read quarterly reports, and track sector trends gain insight into macroeconomic drivers of property returns: interest rate shifts, occupancy dynamics, asset repositioning, and more. This knowledge, while indirect, becomes invaluable when the investor transitions into direct ownership.

Creative entry also means rethinking the idea of ownership itself. In many cases, control is more important than title. Managing a property for a relative, negotiating a rent-to-rent agreement on an underutilised home, or taking responsibility for a vacant unit in exchange for occupancy and a share of profits—these are real investments of time, energy, and risk. They produce decision-making experience, track records, and income. They are not loopholes. They are leverage.

Still, none of these strategies are free from risk. Each comes with unique legal, financial, and operational considerations. Lease options can be voided if improperly drafted. Fractional platforms can suffer from poor governance or illiquidity. Rent-to-rent models can collapse under weak agreements or regulatory non-compliance. House hacking can backfire with the wrong tenant. What separates successful creative investors from opportunists is diligence. They seek legal advice, understand their rights and responsibilities, and approach each structure not as a hack but as a legitimate financial arrangement demanding rigour.

The deeper insight here is that property is not a monolith. It's a constellation of models, strategies, and structures—many of which are accessible well before you meet traditional thresholds of "investor readiness." What matters most at the outset is not ownership for its own sake, but *strategic entry*. The ability to learn while earning. To test hypotheses in real markets. To build competence, not just capital.

Creative entry points are not shortcuts. They are strategic alternatives. They allow you to begin participating in property while building the capacity—financial, intellectual, emotional—to scale. They invite you to ask better questions: *What kind of exposure do I want? What kind of risk can I manage? What is my learning objective at this stage?* And they offer answers that traditional ownership models often obscure.

You do not need to wait to become an investor. You need to reframe what being an investor looks like. Sometimes it means owning the asset. Sometimes it means controlling the income. Sometimes it means learning the system from the inside—quietly, experimentally, and with increasing clarity.

That's where real leverage begins. Not with a large deposit or a pre-approval letter. But with a structure that matches your reality, a strategy that respects your constraints, and a mindset that prizes wisdom over optics. Start there, and you're already investing—whether or not your name is on the deed.

Your First Property Is a Teacher, Not a Trophy

The first property you purchase will likely be your worst-performing asset. That's not a criticism—it's a fact, and often a necessary one. Because the value of that first acquisition lies not in its return on investment, but in its return on insight. The financial metrics may be modest. The process may be clumsy. But the educational dividend can be enormous—if you allow it to be. Yet many new investors approach their first deal as though it were a prize to win, a badge of competence, or a signal to others that they've "made it." This mindset invites pressure, performance, and perfectionism. It chases validation instead of value. And it turns what should be an apprenticeship into a performance.

Treating your first property as a teacher reframes everything. It turns mistakes into case studies. It prioritises understanding over optics. And it frees you from the destructive illusion that your first move must also be your best. This is not a call for mediocrity. It's a call for perspective. Because real estate is not about getting everything right the first time—it's about building durable knowledge through lived experience. And the earliest of those experiences are often the most instructive.

The learning curve in property is steep, not because the underlying principles are complex, but because the variables are numerous—and many only reveal themselves under pressure. You can read a hundred articles about tenant management and still be blindsided by your first dispute. You can memorise checklists and due diligence protocols, only to realise, mid-renovation, that your builder has misquoted the job or your budget hasn't accounted for VAT. These aren't failures of preparation—they're signs that certain lessons cannot be simulated. They must be experienced. And your first property is your classroom.

This means the objective of that first deal is not just profit. It's *exposure*—to the mechanics, the relationships, the constraints, and the decision-making dynamics that define real estate investment in practice. It's your first chance to engage with letting agents, surveyors, tradespeople, legal contracts, mortgage brokers, compliance requirements, and unforeseen costs. It's the space where theory collides with reality—and the consequences, though real, are still containable.

A recurring pattern among seasoned investors is how vividly they remember their first deal—not because of its financial return, but because of what it revealed about their temperament, their blind spots, their assumptions. One investor in Leeds bought a leasehold flat in a mixed-tenure building, lured by the price point and a promising rental yield. Within a year, they were grappling with service charges that doubled, a management company under investigation, and tenants who struggled with noise complaints from the council-owned units below. It was a difficult year. But they learned more about leasehold structures, local housing policy, and tenant screening than any course could have offered. That first deal didn't perform well—but it redefined how they approached every deal thereafter. It made them sharper, more grounded, less reactive.

Contrast that with another investor who spent two years waiting for the "perfect" property—one that hit every metric, ticked every box, and promised immediate positive cash flow. When they finally purchased, the property performed reasonably well, but the investor remained rigid, overly reliant on projections and resistant to market nuance. They lacked the adaptive fluency that only real-world complexity teaches. Their second property was overleveraged and poorly located. Without the humility of earlier feedback, they scaled too fast and ultimately had to unwind part of their portfolio.

The difference between these two paths isn't technical knowledge. It's posture. One approached their first deal as a process. The other, as a performance. The first embraced learning through action. The second deferred learning until it could be done risk-free. But property is not risk-free. And early exposure to manageable mistakes is far less costly than late exposure to high-stakes ones.

This perspective also liberates new investors from the trap of over-optimising. There's a temptation, especially among data-driven professionals, to turn property analysis into a spreadsheet arms race. Every yield must be calculated to the decimal. Every variable modelled. But while rigour is essential, over-modelling can become a form of avoidance. It delays action under the guise of diligence. Your first deal is not the place to execute a perfect model. It's the place to *test* one. To see how your assumptions hold up. To gather your own data. To discover how much yield you actually need to feel secure, how much risk you can tolerate before losing sleep, and how much cash flow is required to maintain interest and commitment.

There's also a broader philosophical point: the property is not the product—you are. Your first deal builds *you*—as an investor, as a strategist, as a problem-solver. The lessons aren't just about ROI, they're about ROE: return on experience. What kind of investor are you becoming? What patterns are you developing? What beliefs are being reinforced? If your first deal is framed as a trophy, these questions are ignored. If it's framed as a teacher, they are front and centre.

Another overlooked benefit of a "teaching" mindset is that it reduces attachment to short-term outcomes. You're less likely to panic during a vacancy or rush a sale during a market dip. You're more likely to analyse your actions objectively and adjust accordingly. And because you're not anchored to the idea of immediate success, you can focus on building the systems—financial, operational, psychological—that make long-term success possible.

Your first property is also a test of your interpersonal skill. Whether you're managing tenants, working with a co-investor, or navigating disputes with a managing agent, you'll learn how you respond to stress, how you communicate under pressure, how you negotiate and compromise. These are soft skills, but they're pivotal. Property is a people business disguised as an asset business. The asset may appreciate on paper, but its real value depends on how well you manage the human variables around it.

None of this is to suggest you should approach your first deal casually. Rigorous research, conservative financial planning, and legal protection are non-negotiables. But the bar should be *sufficient excellence*, not perfection. Your goal is to complete the cycle—acquire, operate, reflect—so that you emerge smarter, calmer, and better positioned for the next move. If the property yields modestly but builds your capability exponentially, it was worth every pound.

Ironically, some of the best long-term portfolios are built by investors who had imperfect first deals. They learned to underwrite more conservatively. They built better reserves. They asked better questions. They stopped outsourcing their judgment to other people's spreadsheets. In other words, they evolved. And that evolution is far more valuable than squeezing an extra 0.5% yield on deal number one.

Perhaps the most dangerous thing a first-time investor can do is treat their first property as proof. Proof that they're smart. That they've arrived. That they belong. This posture leads to defensiveness, inflexibility, and risk denial. But if you treat it as a pilot project—an intentional, bounded experiment with a clear learning agenda—you create space for growth. For iteration. For true understanding.

Letting go of the trophy mentality also helps you resist premature scaling. Many new investors, buoyed by a successful first deal, attempt to replicate too quickly. They apply the same strategy in different markets, or expand into different asset types without recalibrating their systems. But if the first deal was treated as a performance, not a practice, they've built a house on shallow foundations. It's only when the market shifts—interest rates rise, rental demand drops, capital dries up—that the strength of your foundations becomes visible. And your first property, well used, can build those foundations.

Your mindset in that first deal sets the tone for your investment career. It shapes how you view setbacks, how you process information, how you measure progress. If you're willing to see it as a learning laboratory—rich in feedback, demanding in discipline, forgiving in size—you give yourself the best possible start. Not because you'll get everything right, but because you'll learn how to respond when you don't.

That's the real ROI of your first deal. Not the numbers on a spreadsheet, but the investor it begins to shape. Not the trophy you can post online, but the trust you begin to build—in yourself, your process, your principles. And in a field where outcomes are driven less by brilliance than by longevity, that trust is the ultimate asset.

Chapter 3
Choosing Your Strategy—Rent, Flip, or Hold

Every investor, sooner or later, feels the tug of the "best" strategy. The formula with the highest yield, the swiftest turnaround, the neatest tax treatment. But in property, "best" is an empty word unless it is tethered to the person wielding it. The real determinant is fit—the meeting point between method and temperament. To rent, to flip, to hold land—these are not mere tactics. They mirror personality, patience, tolerance for risk, appetite for stress. Numbers alone won't tell you. What matters is how the strategy holds under pressure, how it bends—or breaks—when placed inside the rhythm of your own life. Copying someone else's playbook, without pausing to ask if the beat matches your own, is the surest way to stumble.

This is not a manual comparing rental yields against capital gains. It is something subtler: a guide to choosing with self-awareness. Strategy, in real estate, is personal. Two people can step into the same market, armed with identical capital and knowledge, and walk away with entirely different plans. One may prefer the slow burn of rental accumulation—steady income, growing stability. Another might thrive on the urgency of flipping, relishing the short cycles of buying and selling. A third may take the long, quiet road, purchasing land and waiting for the tide of development to catch up. All three are valid. Each, however, aligns with a different kind of temperament. Knowing yours demands more than research; it requires self-examination.

Identity, in this sense, is the soil in which a strategy takes root. A risk-averse professional with little time and no love for renovations will soon wither in the frantic pace of flipping, no matter how shiny the margins appear. On the other hand, a hands-on problem-solver with design instincts and a trusted contractor at their side may find the slow accrual of rental yields monotonous. These subtleties matter, because property is never passive—despite what glossy seminars suggest. It requires choices, presence, stamina. And a misaligned approach doesn't just underperform; it corrodes energy, breeds resentment, and often drives investors out altogether.

Take renting. It is often celebrated as the safe, sensible path to wealth. And in truth, it can be. A balanced portfolio of rental homes offers recurring income, inflation protection, tax efficiency. But it is also slow, deliberate, heavy with ongoing responsibility. Properties must be stabilised, tenants cared for, roofs patched, boilers replaced. Success comes to those who see patience not as drudgery but as quiet strength. The challenge here is psychological: the grind. Progress is incremental, rarely glamorous. To some, this is deeply rewarding. To others, intolerable.

Flipping, by contrast, seduces with speed. The thrill of fast equity gains, visible transformation, stories worth telling at dinner parties. It attracts those who enjoy sprints more than marathons, who thrive on decisive action and trust their instinct for timing. Yet behind the glamour lies volatility. Deadlines slip, builders go silent, markets cool unexpectedly. Margins vanish in the smallest of miscalculations. The flipper must be both quick and resilient, able to endure compressed bursts of chaos without losing composure. Execution, not theory, makes or breaks the game. Contractors must be managed with rigour—or you become one yourself. Tax rules bite. Financing is tricky. And there is the ever-present risk of mistaking movement for meaning, mistaking a full calendar for a full wallet.

Then there is land, the quiet outlier. It rarely headlines in seminars, but history gives it weight. Land does not yield rent, nor require daily oversight. What it does offer is potential—raw, patient, waiting. When chosen with foresight—near a new motorway, beneath an unannounced rail line, or in a corridor marked for future housing—it can appreciate beyond expectation. But the trade is time. Land ties up capital, generates no cash flow, and may sit dormant for years. It suits those who think in decades, who can bear ambiguity, who do not crave immediate feedback. And yet, it grants a kind of flexibility few other assets offer: develop, partner, rezone, preserve. Quiet power, if you have the patience.

Across these strategies—rent, flip, hold—the common thread is not mechanics but psychology. Rentals ask for steadiness. Flips demand decisiveness. Landholding rewards vision and restraint. Choosing among them is less about tactics than about truth: what kind of investor are you prepared to become? Too many fall into the trap of prestige or peer pressure, mimicking what seems advanced or fashionable. They chase cash flow because it is envied, flips because they trend, land because it sounds sophisticated. But if the temperament doesn't fit, the cost is steep: stress, erratic choices, premature exits.

The wiser path is to pause and count the true costs. Not just the down payment or the projected yield, but the hidden demands: emotional load, time pressure, tolerance for risk. Ask yourself: how much volatility can I stomach? How much patience do I possess? Do I need liquidity soon, or can I wait a decade? Am I energised by managing projects—or exhausted by them? These are not secondary considerations. They are structural. Choose wrong, and the numbers will not save you.

And remember: strategy need not be fixed. You might begin with a flip to generate capital, then shift into rentals for stability. Or hold a parcel of land while running an active portfolio elsewhere. But adaptability only comes from clarity. Without knowing why you chose a path, you will never recognise when it is time to adjust.

This chapter will not only walk through each approach, but also draw out the mindset each demands. It will highlight the places where theory diverges from reality, where investors stumble, and where they recalibrate. It will press you to consider not just what you *can* do, but what you *should* do—given your present resources, your psychology, your time.

Because in property, the "best" strategy is not the one that dazzles on a spreadsheet. It is the one you can return to again and again—sustainably, intelligently, without hollowing out your energy or betraying your principles. Strategy is not about perfect answers. It is about sharper questions, and listening carefully to how your life replies. Let us begin there.

The Identity Behind the Investment

When most new investors approach real estate, they look outward—at yields, comparables, locations, leverage ratios. They hunt for the "right" property or the "most lucrative" strategy, imagining that the secret lies in data or timing. But in truth, the first asset they need to assess is internal. Before choosing whether to flip, rent, or hold land, the question is not "What can I buy?" but *"Who am I as an investor?"* The personality behind the portfolio is not a side note. It's the operating system behind every deal, every decision, and every dollar of risk.

Too often, new investors try to retrofit themselves into someone else's blueprint. They follow an online mentor's house-hacking method, or mimic the aggressive scaling of a YouTube flipper, without examining whether the approach fits their life, risk profile, or deeper goals. This mimicry often leads to burnout—not because the strategy is flawed, but because the person behind it is misaligned. Real estate investing isn't only about what works on paper; it's about what works *for you*—psychologically, practically, and emotionally. A rental portfolio is no good if it keeps you up at night. A flip deal is no win if it breaks your stress threshold. A piece of land is no asset if you're too impatient to wait.

Consider the flipper. Popularised by media and idolised by adrenaline-seeking entrepreneurs, the flipper appears dynamic, decisive, and cash-flow sharp. And yet behind the scenes, flipping demands high bandwidth: sourcing distressed properties, negotiating quickly, managing tradespeople under tight timelines, dealing with regulatory friction, and handling unpredictable cost overruns. If you thrive under pressure, enjoy short bursts of intense project work, and have a keen eye for both design and logistics, flipping might suit you well. But if ambiguity and fast-paced financial swings create anxiety, you may find the volatility unsustainable. The identity of a successful flipper is often forged in the ability to detach emotionally while acting decisively, absorbing risk without losing clarity.

By contrast, rental investing is less thrilling but more methodical. The landlord isn't seeking a dramatic gain; they're constructing a long-term income machine. This strategy favours individuals who value consistency over excitement, who prefer compounding over quick hits, and who can tolerate slow but steady growth. It also demands a certain psychological resilience—the ability to deal with maintenance issues, tenant disputes, late payments, and the occasional vacancy without letting it derail your focus. Good landlords are process thinkers. They develop systems, manage people, and don't get rattled easily. Importantly, they understand that wealth doesn't always look like momentum—it often looks like monotony done well.

Then there's the land investor—the strategist who plays the long game. They may appear inactive, even invisible, during holding periods. But behind that patience is usually a calculated thesis: a future rezoning opportunity, a demographic shift, an infrastructural development plan. Land investors aren't chasing short-term wins. They're creating options: to sell, to develop, to partner, or to preserve. This profile suits the contrarian thinker, the one comfortable with ambiguity, illiquidity, and delayed gratification. But this isn't passive investment. It requires research, vision, and discipline. You need to know what you own, why you own it, and when it might matter. If flipping is a sprint and renting a marathon, landholding is a chess game across generations.

To choose among these paths, you need more than financial calculators. You need self-awareness. What is your real appetite for uncertainty? How much control do you require over your outcomes? Are you more energised by systems or by projects? Do you seek immediate validation or are you comfortable playing the background for years? These aren't abstract musings—they are strategic criteria. Without this introspection, you risk building a portfolio that performs well but *feels wrong*. You'll dread the tasks it demands. You'll second-guess your choices. And at some point, you may walk away—not because the investment failed, but because it failed to fit.

Let's bring this into the real world. Consider two investors, both with £100,000 to deploy. One chooses to buy a small two-bedroom flat, secure a tenant, and build from there. They accept a modest return initially, reinvesting cash flow to maintain the property and slowly build equity. The other takes the same capital and uses it as a deposit to flip a cosmetic fixer-upper, hoping to extract £30,000 in profit within six months. On paper, the second approach might appear more lucrative. But if the investor lacks the time, temperament, or trade network to manage a renovation efficiently, the first path—slow as it may seem—will likely outperform in terms of sustainability and personal fit.

This is not a one-time decision, either. Your investor identity evolves. A young, risk-tolerant professional with low fixed costs may find flipping exhilarating, only to later shift towards rentals as family life demands more stability. Similarly, someone who starts with a rental may eventually use accumulated equity to acquire and hold land as a legacy move. There's no singular path to wealth in real estate—only congruent paths. The skill lies in choosing strategies that match your *current* context and adapting them as your life changes.

It's also worth acknowledging that identity isn't just about temperament—it's also shaped by beliefs. Many investors bring inherited views of money, security, and risk into their decision-making. Perhaps you were raised to fear debt, or to value ownership above all else. Maybe you see property as a tool for liberation, or perhaps as a hedge against instability. These beliefs matter. They act as filters through which you interpret opportunity. But they should not be unexamined. A fear of leverage may protect you—or it may limit your growth. An obsession with cash flow might signal discipline—or it might conceal a discomfort with delayed gratification. Part of becoming a mature investor is learning to interrogate these assumptions, not just follow them.

There is also a cultural layer to identity. In some communities, property ownership is linked to status; in others, to responsibility. In many immigrant households, for instance, real estate symbolises permanence and arrival. In others, it may represent generational burden or a hedge against discriminatory systems. These meanings influence how investors choose to act—and why. A person buying land for preservation is playing a different game from someone buying rental units to fire their boss. Neither is wrong. But confusing their motives would be.

So how do you begin aligning identity with strategy? Start by asking harder questions. Not "What's the best return?" but *"What kind of work do I want to do repeatedly?"* Not "How fast can I scale?" but *"What does success actually look like in my life?"* Ask whether you want to build a lifestyle, a legacy, or simply more liquidity. Ask what you're optimising for—freedom, control, visibility, stability. Then evaluate strategies not in a vacuum but as frameworks that amplify or frustrate those goals.

Investing in real estate is not just an economic act. It's a design choice for your life. The properties you buy become part of your calendar, your psyche, and in many cases, your sense of identity. They will either support or sabotage the version of yourself you're trying to become. That's why identity alignment is not a philosophical luxury. It's a practical necessity. Your temperament will show up in your spreadsheets. Your bandwidth will express itself in your balance sheet. Your values will be reflected in your vacancies.

If you start with this clarity—about who you are, what you want, and how you naturally operate—then the rest becomes strategy. But if you skip this stage, strategy becomes guesswork, and your portfolio becomes a patchwork of half-fit ideas. The best investors aren't those who mimic models. They're the ones who build portfolios that work *with* their lives, not *against* them.

That's the purpose of this subchapter: not to prescribe a winning formula, but to help you locate yourself within the game. To turn inward before acting outward. Because the right investment isn't just a good deal—it's a good fit. And real wealth isn't just measured in returns. It's measured in alignment.

Renting for Steady Growth

Few investment paths promise as much long-term stability as rental property—yet few are so widely misunderstood at the outset. Unlike the allure of flipping or the speculation of land banking, rental real estate invites a quieter kind of commitment. It does not dazzle. It compounds. And because its virtues are understated—predictable income, leveraged equity growth, and tax efficiency—it is often dismissed by those seeking excitement or rapid gains. But for those who can see past the surface, rental property is a vehicle of lasting wealth, made powerful not by speed, but by its capacity for resilience, adaptability, and sustained returns over time.

The common mistake is to equate "passive income" with "effortless income." Rental property is not passive. It is *managed.* Even when you outsource the day-to-day operations to a letting agent, you remain the owner of both the opportunity and the obligation. Toilets break, tenants default, roofs leak, and property taxes fluctuate. Yet these operational frictions, far from being bugs in the system, are actually features—they discourage speculators and reward those who are willing to think structurally. In a marketplace obsessed with immediacy, rental income teaches patience. It slows the pace, not to delay wealth, but to strengthen it.

A well-run rental property produces three kinds of return: cash flow, equity growth through loan amortisation, and market appreciation. Cash flow pays you now. Amortisation builds ownership over time. Appreciation—when and if it comes—creates optionality: to sell, refinance, or leverage into further investment. But none of these returns are guaranteed. They must be cultivated. And the true differentiator between successful landlords and disappointed ones is not the market cycle or mortgage rate—it is *systems thinking*. Sustainable rental portfolios are designed, not discovered.

Consider a two-bedroom terrace in a secondary city—let's say Leeds or Nottingham—purchased for £180,000 with a 75% mortgage. If it rents for £950 per month, after management, insurance, maintenance, and debt servicing, it might yield a modest net cash flow of £150–£200. To the impatient, this seems paltry. But look closer: in five years, the tenant will have repaid a meaningful portion of the loan on your behalf, while the underlying asset may have appreciated by 10–20%—sometimes more in gentrifying pockets. Multiply this by three or four properties, and a portfolio begins to take form not by magic, but by iteration. This is how income becomes infrastructure.

But it only works if you understand what grinds. The daily reality of managing rentals includes vacancy gaps, maintenance emergencies, lease disputes, regulatory compliance, and shifting tenant expectations. One month, it's a boiler replacement; the next, a tenant wants to break their lease early. These are not problems to be eliminated—they are variables to be managed. And for that, you need clarity: about your role, your boundaries, and your bandwidth. Do you want to self-manage, or delegate? Are you ready to handle rent arrears yourself, or would you prefer a managing agent to step in first? These aren't operational questions alone. They're strategic ones.

The quality of your tenant experience is also inseparable from your investment returns. A neglected property invites turnover. Turnover invites cost. Long-term tenants are rarely retained through price alone. They stay when they feel respected, when repairs are handled promptly, when communication is clear. In this sense, being a landlord is not a financial identity—it is a service role. And the better you design that service, the more predictable your income becomes. There's no spreadsheet function for dignity, but its absence will show up eventually in your vacancy rate.

This is not to romanticise renting. There are real limits and risks. Regulatory shifts—such as the abolition of Section 21 in England or the rent control debates in Scotland—can materially alter your strategy. So can macroeconomic forces: rising interest rates, changing demographic patterns, or even pandemics that reshape urban living preferences. But unlike equities or crypto, rental real estate gives you a hands-on lever: you can reconfigure, refinance, redecorate, or retenant. You're not merely exposed to market forces; you are an actor within them. And that agency, when coupled with patience, is what turns volatility into opportunity.

Let's take the example of house hacking—a term now common in investor circles, but often misunderstood. At its core, house hacking means offsetting your living expenses by renting out part of your home. This could be as simple as taking in a lodger, letting a basement flat, or purchasing a multi-unit dwelling and occupying one unit. It's a way to live cheaply while building equity. But more importantly, it is a mindset shift: from consumer to producer, from resident to owner-operator. For many first-time landlords, this small move becomes the ignition point of their portfolio. Not because the cash flow is life-changing—but because the experience is.

That's the deeper truth: your first rental is not just an asset; it's an education. It will teach you about asset management, human psychology, market dynamics, legal frameworks, and your own limits. And if you approach it with the right expectations—not as a shortcut to wealth, but as a foundation for it—you'll build not just a portfolio, but a philosophy. One that prioritises durability over drama, systems over speculation, and long-term gain over short-term noise.

This philosophy also helps inoculate you against one of the most common traps in rental investing: overleveraging in pursuit of speed. Too many aspiring landlords assume that if one property works, ten will work ten times better. They chase rapid expansion, often fuelled by interest-only loans, tight margins, and optimistic forecasts. The result? A fragile portfolio vulnerable to a single missed payment, interest rate hike, or local market downturn. A wiser approach is *measured scaling*: acquiring only when the prior asset is stabilised, reserving capital for contingencies, and treating each property not as a stepping stone but as a stand-alone business.

And finally, there's the question of timing. Rental real estate is unforgiving to the impatient. It takes years for the full benefits of compounding to manifest. But the inverse is also true: time is the greatest ally of the disciplined landlord. Over decades, your tenants pay down your loans, your rents rise with inflation, your equity grows quietly. What looks slow in year one looks smart in year ten. This is the paradox: *the less exciting your rental portfolio feels, the more powerful it probably is.*

So if you're considering rentals, don't ask whether they're exciting. Ask whether they're aligned—with your values, your tolerance, your lifestyle. Ask whether you're willing to embrace the grind in exchange for the growth. Because renting isn't a get-rich-quick scheme. It's a *stay-rich-slowly* framework. And when built with intention, it's one of the most durable, adaptable, and human-scaled strategies in all of property investment.

Flipping Without the Fantasy

Flipping homes has become one of the most mythologised paths in real estate. On screen, it looks effortless: a dilapidated kitchen becomes a magazine spread, a budget miraculously stays intact, and a healthy profit is revealed in dramatic fashion within 30 minutes—complete with triumphant music. Yet beyond the glamourised lens of television and social media lies a far more complex reality: flipping is a business, not a makeover. And as with any business, it carries costs—financial, emotional, and reputational—that are often invisible until you're in the thick of them.

The central misbelief about flipping is that it's simply about buying low and selling high. In truth, that's only the surface-level arithmetic.

The real game is managing margins under pressure: accounting for the true cost of capital, controlling the variability of renovation, navigating planning permissions, dealing with contractors and inspectors, and timing the market—all while under relentless financial and logistical constraints. To succeed consistently, one must be as much a project manager as an investor, and as comfortable with spreadsheets as with skip hire and scaffolding.

A typical flip timeline might run six to twelve months, from acquisition to resale. But every additional week of holding reduces your return, especially if you're using bridging finance or short-term commercial loans—tools that come with high interest rates and tight repayment windows. Suppose you purchase a property for £180,000, budget £40,000 in renovations, and aim to sell it at £270,000. On paper, you expect a £50,000 profit. But now factor in legal fees, stamp duty, contractor overruns, additional surveyor reports, skipped council inspections, property insurance, utilities, and marketing costs. Add in an extra month or two of holding during a slow market. Suddenly that profit can erode by half—or vanish entirely. And this is assuming the resale valuation holds, which is not guaranteed in a volatile or oversupplied market.

The risk profile intensifies for those who mistake aesthetic improvement for value creation. A new kitchen may impress, but if you haven't addressed structural issues, updated wiring, or improved insulation in a region where EPC ratings now influence buyer decisions, your property may linger unsold. Cosmetic flips, while visually gratifying, rarely yield consistent premiums unless paired with substantive upgrades or clever repositioning in the market. Buyers today are more informed—and more sceptical—than ever.

There are, however, flips that work. But they work because of *discipline*, not drama. The most successful flippers operate with military precision: they know their neighbourhood data intimately, maintain longstanding relationships with reliable tradespeople, and execute each phase of the project according to strict timelines and margin targets. They walk away from deals that don't fit their model, even if the property is charming or the vendor desperate. They plan for worst-case scenarios—flood risk assessments, asbestos discoveries, drainage complications—rather than hoping everything will run to schedule. Their key advantage is not vision, but *rigour.*

Consider the experience of a developer in Bristol who purchased a Victorian semi-detached in need of extensive work. The plan was to convert it into two high-end flats within nine months. But after discovery of dry rot in the joists, additional planning approval required for changes to the façade, and delays in material supply during a construction backlog, the project stretched to sixteen months. Profit margins were cut by over 60%. And yet, the flip did not fail entirely—because the investor had built buffers into their budget, refused to rush the valuation process, and kept contingency cash aside. Their recalibration wasn't a retreat; it was an evolution of their flipping strategy from reactive to resilient.

Not all stories end so diplomatically. A novice flipper in Manchester, lured by the idea of "cheap" housing stock, bought a three-bedroom terrace at auction for £95,000, aiming to spend £20,000 in updates and flip it for £150,000. They hadn't accounted for the property's inclusion in a poorly performing school catchment, local crime rates affecting buyer confidence, or the substandard plumbing that had to be completely redone. By the time the property was ready, the market had cooled. It eventually sold for £138,000—barely covering costs, let alone the dozens of unpaid hours invested. The investor didn't lose everything, but they walked away with one lesson: *buying cheap is not the same as buying smart.*

Flipping also has psychological implications that are often glossed over. The speed and intensity of a flip can distort decision-making. Investors become emotionally attached to their projects, unwilling to compromise on listing price because they "know how much work went into it." Or they overcapitalise on features they personally love but that add little to market value. Others fall prey to sunk cost fallacies, pouring more money into a deal that no longer makes sense, simply because they're "too far in to back out." A wise flipper cultivates detachment. You are not the owner of a masterpiece—you are the operator of a margin-driven asset.

And then there is the ethical dimension. In areas experiencing rapid gentrification, flipping has been linked—fairly or not—to displacement, rent inflation, and hollowed-out communities. While not every flip contributes to this dynamic, responsible investors must be mindful of their impact. Are you enhancing housing stock or simply exploiting arbitrage? Are your renovations improving energy efficiency and safety, or just aesthetic appeal? Are you pricing for aspirational buyers who actually want to live in the area, or creating speculative pressure that displaces local families? These questions don't have tidy answers—but they matter.

Flipping can be a powerful short-term wealth generator, but it demands a level of skill, discipline, and temperament that most beginners underestimate. It is not a shortcut; it is a business model. And like all businesses, it must be built on data, not instinct; process, not passion. Before you attempt your first flip, ask yourself: do I have the infrastructure to manage timelines, contractors, financing, and compliance? Do I understand the granular economics of the neighbourhood I'm operating in? Do I have enough margin—financially and psychologically—to handle surprises?

If you don't yet, that's fine. It doesn't mean you shouldn't flip. But it does mean you should treat your first project not as a profit centre, but as a pilot. Go smaller than you think. Build partnerships with experienced trades. Document every decision. Run detailed post-mortems, whether the result is a win or a wash. In this way, even a break-even flip becomes a platform for compound learning—about markets, about money, and about yourself.

There is no shame in the slow flip. A conservative approach, marked by modest upgrades and targeted resale to a well-understood buyer profile, can yield better returns than a grand vision undermined by chaos. Real value is not created in how much you spend on tiles or how quickly you can stage a listing—it's in how well you manage risk. That's the hidden discipline behind successful flipping: risk management disguised as renovation.

So strip away the fantasy. Understand the math, respect the grind, and anchor every decision in disciplined realism. Flipping is not for everyone—but done wisely, it is not just about making money. It is about building a practice of judgement, foresight, and control that can sharpen your edge as an investor, long after the paint has dried.

The Case for Dirt: Land as a Legacy Play

Land is the oldest asset class known to civilisation, yet it remains one of the most misunderstood in the modern property investor's toolkit. While homes, flats, and commercial buildings command headlines and dominate first-time investor conversations, land—unbuilt, raw, and often unglamorous—sits in the background, quietly accruing value. It doesn't cash flow like a rental. It doesn't transform overnight like a flip. But for those willing to think generationally rather than transactionally, land represents not just a speculative punt or passive holding, but a foundational asset: resilient, strategic, and deeply consequential.

What makes land so enduring is also what makes it opaque to many new investors. Its value isn't always visible, and its potential isn't always immediate. Unlike a house with doors, walls, and rent-paying tenants, a plot of land may appear static. But beneath that stillness is a slow-burning alchemy driven by location, policy, infrastructure, and time. *Land is not valuable because of what it is—but because of what it can become.* This difference in value logic makes land investment a mental reframe: you are not buying income; you are buying optionality.

Understanding zoning is central to this reframe. Every parcel of land exists within a legal framework that determines what can and cannot be built upon it. These planning designations—residential, commercial, agricultural, green belt, or mixed-use—are not merely bureaucratic categories; they are economic levers. A shift in zoning can transform a plot's value overnight, often without a single spade hitting the soil. Savvy land investors study local development plans, monitor political changes, and anticipate where infrastructure projects (motorways, schools, hospitals, railway stations) may trigger rezoning. Their profit isn't manufactured through renovations or marketing but through *positioning*—being early to where the future is quietly arriving.

A case study worth noting is the expansion corridor outside Cambridge, where agricultural plots purchased for less than £10,000 per acre in the early 2000s skyrocketed to £250,000+ per acre after infrastructure investment and zoning revisions aligned with university-led development. These gains weren't speculative lottery wins; they were the result of disciplined research, patience, and landowners who understood that local politics could be as financially consequential as interest rates.

However, land is not only for those playing the planning game. There are forms of land investment that rely on more defensive logic: *holding*, rather than developing. For example, farmland has historically outperformed many commercial real estate sectors in periods of economic uncertainty. In part, this is because its value is underpinned by intrinsic utility—food production—rather than consumer demand or corporate leasing cycles. In the UK, farmland also carries significant tax advantages, including Inheritance Tax relief under Agricultural Property Relief, making it a strategic component in multi-generational estate planning. For families looking to preserve wealth and pass it forward intact, land is not a vanity asset—it's a legacy mechanism.

This perspective broadens the concept of "return." When measured only in yield or appreciation, land can appear underwhelming. But when viewed through the lens of control, stewardship, and long-horizon value, it becomes a radically different proposition. A well-situated piece of land offers the investor control over its future use, the flexibility to lease, develop, hold, or donate, and the potential to shape local outcomes. This isn't theoretical. Increasing numbers of impact-minded investors are acquiring greenfield sites for preservation or ecological restoration, treating land not just as a financial asset but a cultural and environmental statement. It's wealth not just stored, but *anchored.*

And yet, land investment is not without its unique risks. Liquidity is chief among them. Unlike a rental property that can be sold to a wide audience, undeveloped land typically appeals to a narrower buyer pool. Sales can take longer, valuations can vary wildly based on future-use assumptions, and in downturns, land values can be the first to stall. Moreover, financing land is harder: many banks are unwilling to lend on non-income-producing property, which means investors must often use cash or seek specialist financing, which carries higher rates and stricter terms. The lack of leverage, while preserving safety, also reduces immediate scalability.

This is why *time horizon* is the defining variable in land investing. Those seeking quick wins are likely to be disappointed. But those with five-, ten-, or twenty-year outlooks are operating in a different risk-reward matrix. They can absorb the time it takes for urban sprawl to reach their site, for planning regimes to evolve, or for demographic trends to catch up with their geographic thesis. Their edge is not access to capital—it's the willingness to wait.

A common misstep is assuming that land is the exclusive domain of large institutions or high-net-worth individuals. While it's true that prime land is expensive, the market is far more layered than many realise. Small plots—garden extensions, paddocks, brownfield infill lots, or residual land beside railway lines—can often be acquired at entry-level prices and offer opportunities for micro-development, planning gain, or strategic resale. The key is not size but *context.* A quarter-acre in a transitional postcode, if correctly rezoned or aggregated with adjacent plots, can be more valuable than five acres in the wrong postcode with rigid restrictions.

Another path is co-ownership. Savvy investors sometimes pool resources to acquire larger parcels that are individually unaffordable but collectively strategic. This approach requires legal precision—through structured joint ventures or land syndicates—but it lowers the barrier to entry and spreads risk. And crucially, it allows younger investors or those without six-figure capital reserves to gain exposure to a historically high-performing asset class.

Then there's the regulatory dimension. Investors must stay alert to changes in local planning frameworks, compulsory purchase schemes, environmental protections, and community objections. A promising parcel can become a planning quagmire if one fails to consult properly, engage with local councils, or address ecological concerns. Good land investors don't just look at maps; they attend council meetings, build relationships with planners, and stay immersed in the shifting landscape of regulation and sentiment.

Finally, land forces a different kind of investor psychology—one that prizes *restraint* over action. In residential property, there is constant activity: tenants to manage, repairs to oversee, income to count. Land requires trust in deferred value. You may hold it for years before any monetary benefit appears. This stillness is not inactivity—it's accumulation. The investor's job is to hold the asset in place while the world evolves around it. Roads are built. Populations shift. Markets expand. And when timing aligns with vision, land delivers.

What makes land compelling is not just its financial upside but its conceptual elegance. It is the only real estate asset that exists before, beyond, and often in spite of architecture. It asks you to zoom out, to widen your field of vision from the quarter to the decade. It rewards patience, diligence, and an ability to think spatially and politically. And in an investment world increasingly obsessed with fast returns and flashy outcomes, it invites a different kind of ambition—one rooted in stewardship, in foresight, and in the quiet confidence that real value doesn't need to shout.

Chapter 4
The Psychology of Property Decisions

No spreadsheet, however sophisticated, can tell you everything that matters about a property. Nor will it whisper in your ear when your confidence is misplaced, when instinct has slipped its bearings, or when emotion is scribbling cheques your future self may struggle to honour. For all its data points and due diligence, property investing is never just arithmetic. It is steeped in psychology—shaped by fear, hope, ego, memory, and identity. To grasp that isn't a soft indulgence. It's a competitive edge.

This chapter is not concerned with the mechanics of reading markets or calculating rental yields. Its focus is subtler: how to read yourself. Every decision carries an unseen emotional freight—the dream of the "perfect" home, the dread of missing out, the weight of financial exposure, the thrill of control, the scars of past mistakes. Left unexamined, these forces sabotage even the soundest logic. Confronted head-on, they become levers you can work with. And mastering them is what separates opportunists from disciplined wealth-builders.

There is no such thing as an investment untainted by feeling. This is especially true for first-timers, whose choices so often double as a referendum on identity. That initial deal is rarely about bricks and mortar alone; it is about proving something. Am I capable? Decisive? Financially grown? Will this vindicate me in the eyes of my peers, my parents, myself? Such internal questions distort the lens through which one evaluates opportunity. Evidence bends to desire.

Emotional self-regulation is among the least celebrated but most critical skills in property. The ability to pause when urgency spikes. To notice when attraction clouds appraisal. To name fear instead of acting from it. This is not softness—it is steel. Investors without it stumble into sunk cost traps, confuse boldness for wisdom, mistake busy motion for real progress. Those who cultivate it tend to move more slowly, but also more surely. They miss fewer fundamentals, recover faster, and—crucially—last longer.

Advice pours from every corner today. Online platforms, social feeds, slick influencers—all dispensing frameworks, formulas, "no-fail" checklists. But rarely do they teach how to think, or how to feel one's way wisely. Yet intuition—trained properly—is among the finest tools in an investor's kit. Misunderstood, it is dangerous. Gut instinct, shaped by experience and reflection, becomes pattern recognition. Gut instinct, fuelled by desperation or vanity, is a liability.

The brain craves logic; the gut craves safety. And the two often collide. A property may tick every analytical box, yet if it lies in a neighbourhood you cannot read, or stirs a vague unease, the body whispers caution. Conversely, you may be instantly drawn to a place that flatters your aspirational identity but fails even basic investment criteria. The art lies in holding both impulses in tension—neither dismissing nor blindly obeying. This balance only matures with deals done, and it asks for humility.

Nowhere is this conflict sharper than in the paralysis before a first major purchase. This is not mere dithering. It is a cocktail of financial anxiety, cognitive overload, and social comparison. Move too quickly and you fear looking naïve; wait too long and you feel weak. Suddenly every "for sale" sign becomes cosmic symbolism, every hesitation a character flaw. Yet progress in property is not about striking a flawless pose. It is about establishing a rhythm. Confidence does not precede the first deal; it is forged in the doing—with safeguards in place.

Sometimes, the most astute move is to decline. Novices often conflate action with advancement. Yet restraint is a mark of maturity. Walking away from a near-miss feels anticlimactic, but it is victory nonetheless. Saying no, from clarity rather than fear, shows that your strategy has backbone, that standards are firm, that you will not pad your portfolio with compromises destined to sour. Opportunities are abundant; your capital and your reputation are not.

And saying no extends beyond bad deals. It includes bad timing, misaligned partners, misguided motives. Some properties arrive dressed with subtle lures: the house that echoes your childhood, the neighbourhood that mirrors your imagined self, the fixer-upper that promises redemption. These emotional hooks seduce, but they often conceal hard flaws. If the maths fails, or the risk jars with your life stage, discipline demands you release it. Even when it stings. Especially then.

Perhaps the most insidious trap is attachment. It creeps in gently. You visit the same open house three times. You begin sketching layouts, imagining paint colours, tenants, transformations. The fantasy runs ahead of the facts. Now walking away feels like loss, though the numbers say otherwise. This is sunk cost at its purest—not just money, but narrative. Rationalising replaces analysing. You guard the dream rather than the capital.

Awareness, though, is a potent antidote. Naming the trap—"I'm clinging to the story I've spun"—creates a gap between self and decision. It recentres you on strategy, not infatuation. It permits you to be both human and rigorous. The best investors don't exile emotion; they integrate it. They know property is personal. Every square metre holds psychological weight as well as economic promise. They don't deny it—they account for it.

What follows in this chapter is an excavation of those inner mechanics. Not only what you *should* think, but how you actually do think when money, meaning, and risk collide. We'll look at cautionary tales where unchecked emotion wrecked a deal—and others where intuition proved a quiet saviour. We'll examine the fears that hobble first-timers, and why the mind so often urges us towards the wrong purchase for the "right" reason. Most of all, we'll equip you with tools to move through doubt—not by erasing it, but by understanding its voice.

Psychological sophistication is not about numbness. It is about emotional intelligence under strain. Property decisions will test your judgement, your relationships, even your sense of self. Yet these same tests, rightly understood, sharpen instincts, refine values, and help you build not merely a sturdier portfolio but a sturdier self. What you learn about markets entwines with what you learn about your own limits—of risk, of patience, of desire.

If the spreadsheet serves as map, then psychology is the compass. And knowing how to read both is what ensures you do not merely arrive, but arrive intact—with assets aligned to your aims, and decisions you can own without regret.

Buying with Both Brain and Gut:

There is a moment in nearly every serious property investor's life when they stand inside a potential acquisition—perhaps it's a slightly overpriced two-bedroom flat in a gentrifying postcode, or an underloved corner terrace with poor lighting and great bones—and feel an inexplicable pull. The spreadsheets don't quite add up. The agent is cagey. The numbers hover on the edge of logic. Yet something feels *right.* Or, perhaps more pressingly, something feels *wrong.* And it's in this moment—the quiet intersection between analysis and instinct—that the real investor emerges.

Property decisions are rarely made on data alone. Nor should they be. Real estate is a human field, deeply embedded in memory, aspiration, and place. It's not just a financial play—it's a spatial and emotional one. And while the language of investing leans heavily on rationalism—ROI, yield, cap rate, LTV ratios—the actual decision-making process is far less sterile. Emotions are present, whether acknowledged or not. What separates the successful from the short-sighted is not the absence of feeling but the *integration* of emotion into a robust, disciplined framework.

There's a cultural bias in financial circles that suggests intuition is unscientific, or worse, dangerous. But this is a misreading of both psychology and experience. Intuition is not guesswork. It is pattern recognition—an internal synthesis of past experience, subtle cues, and stored knowledge that often operates below the level of conscious reasoning. The problem arises when instinct is mistaken for impulsiveness. Untrained gut reactions can lead you into speculative traps, vanity buys, or emotional overreach. But *trained intuition*, built through reflective practice and continuous learning, can flag red flags faster than any spreadsheet and spotlight opportunities others miss.

The key is knowing when your gut is wise and when it's wounded. This distinction requires rigorous self-inquiry. Are you hesitating because the deal doesn't make sense—or because you're afraid of commitment? Are you drawn to a property because it reminds you of something nostalgic—or because you've done the research and see a clear trajectory for value growth? Untangling these signals is what turns emotional noise into strategic insight.

A seasoned investor is not someone who has silenced emotion. It's someone who has learned how to interrogate it. For instance, let's say you walk away from a deal that your spreadsheet tells you is solid, but your body tenses every time you revisit it. That tension may be telling you something crucial—perhaps you're entering a location you don't understand, or working with a seller whose ethics are questionable. Your discomfort, if explored honestly, can become a diagnostic tool. Conversely, unchecked excitement can be just as dangerous. Many investors have fallen in love with properties that matched their personal aesthetic or lifestyle goals but failed every practical test of cash flow, maintenance risk, and tenant demand. The gut needs a counterpart—the brain—to ground it in reality.

This doesn't mean every decision should be slow or paralysed by overthinking. Some of the best acquisitions are made swiftly—but not rashly. Speed can coexist with clarity. The trick is to prepare in advance: define your criteria, know your limits, understand your financial profile, study the market. When you've done that homework, your intuitive response in the moment becomes sharper, more reliable. You're no longer guessing—you're accessing embodied knowledge.

Let's take a practical example. A couple—first-time buyers turned novice investors—find a small unit on a back street near a rapidly regenerating station hub. It's grimy, tenanted by students, poorly staged. On paper, the yield looks passable but not exciting. But something about the street pattern, the neighbouring infrastructure upgrades, and a handful of planning applications spotted on the local council portal sparks interest. The couple have walked this area for months. They've tracked rental data. Their gut says this unit, while unimpressive now, sits in a corridor of potential. They move. Three years later, it doubles in value. Was that luck? Perhaps partly. But it was also pattern recognition, grounded in lived observation—*a gut backed by informed judgement.*

Compare that with another investor who buys a refurbished two-up-two-down in a town they don't know, dazzled by Instagram-worthy finishes and a persuasive agent pitch. They stretch their budget, driven by FOMO and the allure of fast returns. The deal closes. Six months later, the tenancy turns over twice, maintenance costs spike, and the local job market starts to dip. The investor realises they bought a fantasy, not a strategy. Their gut told them it felt glamorous; their brain never got to weigh in.

These contrasting cases illustrate a central point: you need both faculties engaged. Numbers matter. So does narrative. Successful property investing is less like chess and more like poker—a game of probability, psychology, and calibrated risk. You'll never have perfect information. But you can build a reliable inner compass that blends logic with experience, research with instinct.

And the more deals you review—whether you act on them or not—the sharper that compass becomes. Reviewing properties without the pressure to act helps you practise detachment. Walking away becomes easier. You stop falling for the perfect kitchen or the "off-market exclusive." You start asking smarter questions: What's the true driver of demand in this location? Where are the long-term employment trends? What do local planning frameworks suggest about the neighbourhood's future shape? And crucially—how does this opportunity sit with my values, my time horizon, and my risk appetite?

This alignment is often what gives investors peace of mind—not just the financial returns. When your purchases reflect your worldview, your schedule, your financial psychology—you stop treating real estate like a competition, and start treating it like a craft. You become less reactive, more strategic. You begin to enjoy the work of discernment. And your investment decisions start to reflect not just market timing, but personal truth.

There's also a case to be made for knowing when not to decide. When your instinct and your intellect are misaligned, pause. When the data is compelling but you feel a quiet disquiet, pause. When everything looks perfect but you're rushing because of external pressure, pause. These moments of suspension are not weak. They are wise. They signal that you are respecting the weight of your decisions. That you are not just buying a property—you are making a declaration about how you want your time, money, and energy to be used.

Real estate investing, at its best, is not just a way to grow capital. It is a vehicle for learning. And every decision—right or wrong—becomes a mirror. Over time, you learn what kinds of pressure distort your thinking. You learn where your biases lie—toward familiarity, novelty, prestige, or perceived safety. You begin to see which cues you can trust and which temptations you must resist. *This is how intuition is shaped: not by guesswork, but by reflective practice.*

Buying with both brain and gut is not easy. It's a skill that gets stronger the more you challenge it, the more you review your mistakes, and the more you respect both data and feeling as valid sources of insight. It requires self-trust—not the naive kind that says, "I know best," but the cultivated kind that says, "I've done the work to earn this instinct." That's the mindset of the long-term investor. Not reactive, not romantic, but grounded. Astute. Calm under pressure.

This subchapter is your invitation to develop that mindset with intention. Not by choosing between rationality and emotion, but by weaving them together into a strategic whole. What you'll discover is not only how to make better property decisions—but how to become the kind of person whose very thinking is an asset.

Fear of the First Deal:

There's a peculiar kind of dread that shadows the first-time property investor—not the abstract fear of losing money, but something more insidious: the paralysis of possibility. When you've never owned an asset, every decision feels existential. You analyse spreadsheets until your eyes blur. You watch prices move in real time, convinced the market is conspiring against you. You read books, compare interest rates, attend webinars, calculate contingencies, then restart the process—only more anxiously this time. Behind all of this effort is not laziness or indifference but a deep, often unspoken worry: *What if I get this wrong?*

This fear is rarely about risk in its purest financial sense. It's psychological. It's reputational. It's personal. The first deal doesn't just feel like a purchase—it feels like a test of competence, maturity, even identity. People hesitate not because they lack information, but because information alone can't guarantee certainty. Behavioural psychologists call this the *action-intention gap*: the disconnect between what we know and what we do. We believe in the logic of property. We see others doing it successfully. Yet our own hands remain frozen.

There's a reason for this. From a cognitive standpoint, first-time investment decisions trigger multiple internal systems—many of which evolved not for prudent analysis but for survival. Risk activates the amygdala, the brain's fear centre, which is notoriously bad at assessing modern threats. It can't distinguish between the danger of an overvalued duplex and the threat of a predator in tall grass. To the primitive brain, both suggest: *don't move.* Add to this the modern overlays of financial shame, social comparison, and digital noise, and hesitation becomes not only predictable but almost inevitable.

But hesitation is not always irrational. In fact, it can be a form of wisdom. It signals that something matters. That your money, time, and energy are finite—and that you're not interested in gambling them lightly. The challenge is not to eliminate hesitation but to interrogate it. *What am I actually afraid of?* Losing money? Looking foolish? Making a permanent mistake? Committing to something that locks me into an identity I'm not sure I want? These are all valid fears. But they demand to be examined, not obeyed.

This is where psychological precision becomes critical. One of the most common traps for first-time investors is confusing uncertainty with danger. Just because a deal can't be predicted with complete confidence doesn't mean it's a bad decision. No property investment is guaranteed. But uncertainty does not automatically equal recklessness. The goal, then, is to shift the internal narrative from "What if I fail?" to "What am I prepared to learn?"

Framing the first deal as a definitive judgment is paralysing. Framing it as a strategic experiment is empowering. The best investors treat their early moves not as declarations of genius but as apprenticeships. They know they'll make errors. They budget for them—not just financially but emotionally. What separates those who act from those who circle indefinitely is not blind courage, but calibrated humility. They know the risk, and they step forward anyway—not because they're sure, but because they're ready to *grow* through the doing.

One practical tool here is behavioural pre-commitment. Define your criteria and your limits before you're emotionally invested. For instance: "I will only buy if the cash-on-cash return is above 6%, the neighbourhood has at least 5 years of stable demand indicators, and I've spoken to two local agents and one current landlord in the area." These rules, set before urgency or temptation distorts judgement, provide a safety scaffold. They let you say no with clarity—and yes with confidence.

There's also value in timeboxing your decision window. Endless analysis is a form of avoidance. Set a timeline: 30 days to research, 30 days to view properties, 30 days to make an offer. This doesn't guarantee success, but it introduces productive constraint. When decision-making stretches indefinitely, risk gets distorted, fear compounds, and motivation depletes. Progress—any progress—becomes impossible.

Another overlooked factor is the role of social reinforcement. Many new investors make the mistake of confiding only in friends or family who are unfamiliar with the realities of property. These voices, often well-meaning, can amplify doubt: "Are you sure the market isn't crashing?" "Isn't this a bad time to buy?" "What if your tenants destroy the place?" Without perspective, these questions sound like truths. But when you immerse yourself—even casually—in communities of active investors, you normalise risk. You hear about setbacks, but also about wins. You learn that making an imperfect first deal is often better than waiting indefinitely for the perfect one.

Of course, this doesn't mean leaping blindly. There's a difference between boldness and bravado. The antidote to fear is not swagger—it's structure. It's knowing how the numbers work. Understanding the leverage dynamics. Doing the work to model downside scenarios. Learning how to screen a tenant. Studying what to look for in a good building survey. Confidence isn't manufactured—it's built, step by step, by confronting the unknown and doing your due diligence.

Consider a real example. A new investor in Birmingham spent nine months analysing local markets. He'd saved for years, knew his target yield, had read every book on buy-to-let strategy. Still, he hadn't made a move. What finally tipped him into action wasn't another spreadsheet—it was a frank conversation with a mentor who said: "You've done enough to survive a mistake. So stop trying to avoid all mistakes." He bought a modest two-bedroom flat in a walkable area, slightly above his budget but well below local averages. Twelve months later, the rent was steady, the value modestly up, and—more importantly—he was no longer stuck.

That's the real pivot. The purpose of your first deal is not to get rich—it's to get *unstuck*. To begin. To test your assumptions. To see how you think under pressure. To make mistakes while the stakes are still manageable. The worst that usually happens is not financial ruin—it's minor miscalculation. The best that happens is transformation: you become someone who no longer hesitates to act when others freeze. And that identity shift is worth far more than a few extra basis points on yield.

Let's also be candid about the risks of *not* acting. Over time, chronic indecision becomes its own liability. The longer you sit out, the more you fear missing out. The more the market moves, the more bitterly you watch it. And eventually, you risk swinging too far the other way—making a rushed, compensatory purchase driven by emotion, not insight. Avoiding the first deal because you fear making a bad one can paradoxically increase the odds that your first deal *is* a bad one—because it's born of frustration, not clarity.

A healthier mindset is to accept that your first deal will be *imperfect.* That's not a flaw—it's a feature. Every experienced investor carries stories of naive buys, underbudgeted refurbs, or tenant headaches. But they also carry something more powerful: *momentum.* They learned what to ask next time. What to research better. What clauses to include in a contract. They didn't wait to be perfect—they acted, reflected, adjusted, and improved.

And the ability to do that—to act despite uncertainty, to learn in real time—is the core skill of any long-term investor. Property markets are dynamic. Economic cycles shift. Regulation evolves. You won't be able to foresee every scenario. But you can develop the resilience and strategic agility to navigate whatever emerges. And that process begins not with knowledge alone, but with the decision to *do* something with it.

Fear, ultimately, is not the enemy. Stagnation is. The goal is not to suppress doubt but to outgrow it—through action, not abstraction. Your first deal will teach you more than any course or consultant. It won't be your best deal. It shouldn't be. But it will be your most important—because it turns you from someone who studies property into someone who *owns* property. From an observer into a participant. From potential into actual.

That transformation is worth the discomfort. Not because it's easy, but because it's essential. And once you've made it, you'll look back and wonder why you waited so long.

Learning to Walk Away

The most powerful decision a new investor can make is not always to act, but to abstain. In a culture obsessed with hustle, acquisition, and the public parade of success, restraint is often confused with indecision. But among the most seasoned property investors—those who've survived downturns, market manias, and personal misjudgements—the ability to walk away is not just respected; it's revered. This is not a virtue for the timid, but a core skill for the wise. In real estate, where the stakes often run into six or seven figures and where the wrong choice can lock up years of opportunity cost, the discipline to decline can determine the shape of a career far more than the eagerness to transact.

The psychological pull toward action is deeply human. Behavioural economists have long studied the "action bias"—our innate tendency to prefer doing something over doing nothing, especially when under pressure. On the football pitch, this is the goalkeeper who dives preemptively during a penalty kick, even though statistical analysis suggests they'd stop more goals by remaining centred. In real estate, it's the novice investor who feels that unless they buy now—this week, this month—they'll be left behind, edged out by savvier peers or swallowed by a rising market. But sound investing is not a race against time. It's a choreography with risk, capital, and context. *Saying no is not a delay—it's a decision.*

Deals are seductive. A freshly-listed duplex in a "gentrifying" postcode. A fixer-upper with "unrealised potential." A pre-auction whisper from a friend of a friend with inside access. The language surrounding property investing is deliberately persuasive: off-market, below value, high yield, value-add. But in reality, most properties are not bargains; most "opportunities" are not unique. The market is not whispering to you. It's testing your discernment. And it does so most aggressively when your confidence is lowest or your ambitions are highest. At the start of your investing life, you are particularly vulnerable—either to overconfidence, stemming from too much theory and too little experience, or to desperation, driven by the need to prove that you belong in the game.

Walking away requires more than data. It demands a mindset that prioritises clarity over closure. Consider this: a property may tick all your analytical boxes—reasonable price per square metre, solid rental demand, acceptable yield—but still not be right for you. Why? Because investment success is not just about the asset. It's about *alignment.* With your capacity, with your goals, with your temperament. If a property will consume more time than you can afford, expose you to partners you don't trust, or put you at odds with your sleep, it's not a good deal. It's a distraction wearing a spreadsheet.

There is also the trap of sunken effort. You may have already spent hours running the numbers, booked multiple inspections, perhaps even paid for a survey or valuation. The more effort you've invested, the harder it becomes to detach. This is the sunk cost fallacy in action: the psychological bias that makes us throw good money—or time—after bad, simply because we've already committed. Smart investors inoculate themselves against this by setting *deal breakers* in advance. These are not just price ceilings or cash flow thresholds, but qualitative boundaries: If the vendor refuses transparency. If the local council zoning is ambiguous. If your gut says something feels off. These are not soft signals; they are decision architecture.

The most underappreciated cost of a bad deal is not the capital lost, but the time and optionality foregone. While you're nursing a poorly performing property, navigating conflict with co-investors, or untangling legal and regulatory missteps, *better opportunities are passing you by.* The market always moves. Capital is finite. Your attention is a scarce resource. The wrong deal, especially early on, doesn't just set you back—it erodes your investing identity. Instead of becoming someone who acts with clarity and precision, you risk becoming reactive, defensive, or cynical. And cynicism, while fashionable in markets, is just fear in a suit.

One of the most seasoned investors I've worked with, a woman who built a £25 million portfolio over two decades, shared a simple mantra: *"If I don't feel peaceful before the contract, I walk."* Peace, in this context, doesn't mean certainty. No deal is ever risk-free. But it means congruence—between the numbers and your values, between your ambitions and your actual bandwidth. She once passed on a central London property that was aggressively undervalued due to probate complications. On paper, it was gold. But the family dispute behind it made her uneasy. Months later, it emerged that the title was contested, and the buyer who pounced is still locked in legal purgatory. *Knowing when not to act saved her more than any spreadsheet ever could.*

Walking away is also cultural. In many investing communities, there's a badge of honour in "making things work." But that badge can become a blindfold. Just because something *can* be wrangled into profitability doesn't mean *you* are the right person to do it, or that now is the time. The notion that success lies solely in resilience is incomplete. Equally important is strategic abstention: the courage to reserve your capital, your energy, and your conviction for something that truly fits.

Learning to walk away is not an argument for passivity. It's a call to maturity. To understand that every "no" clears the way for a more aligned "yes." That discernment compounds, just like capital. And that the best investors don't collect properties—they curate them. Each acquisition is a deliberate addition to a long-term vision, not a reaction to market noise, peer pressure, or internal doubt.

As a practical skill, walking away can be trained. Build into your investment process a final review step that asks not just, *Can I afford this?* but, *Does this deal respect my boundaries?* Keep a "cooling off" period between due diligence and decision. Use a second set of eyes—a mentor, a peer, a legal adviser—to challenge your enthusiasm with scepticism. Create a space in your calendar not just for action, but for *reflection.* Real estate rewards the bold, yes. But it equally rewards the patient, the precise, and the principled.

In the landscape of property investing, walking away isn't failure. It's filtration. It's how you sharpen your edge. The longer you're in the game, the more you'll realise that the deals you *don't* do are often the ones that protect your future the most. Because this game is not about winning once—it's about staying in it long enough to let wisdom, rather than urgency, build your portfolio.

Sunk Costs and Emotional Attachments

Few mistakes in property investment are as quietly destructive as staying committed to a bad deal because you've already committed too much. Whether the currency is time, money, reputation, or imagination, the psychology is the same: *we confuse investment with destiny*. This is the trap of sunk costs—when past expenditures distort present reasoning—and it collides with one of the most emotionally volatile landscapes in investing: real estate. Unlike stocks, property is physical, visible, inhabitable. You can stand in it. Dream in it. Argue in front of it with your spouse. It's this tangibility that makes it a uniquely dangerous canvas for emotional attachment, especially when paired with ego, nostalgia, or hope masquerading as analysis.

The sunk cost fallacy is well-documented in behavioural economics. We resist abandoning a course of action if we've already put significant effort or resources into it—even when that action is demonstrably no longer beneficial. This bias infects even seasoned professionals. In real estate, it takes many forms: continuing with a renovation project that's far over budget, holding onto an underperforming rental because it's "almost" turned around, or refusing to admit that a location you believed in five years ago is simply not what the market values today. What unites these errors is not poor data, but *compromised decision-making frameworks*—ones that confuse persistence with prudence.

Part of the problem is that real estate invites personal narrative. You don't just buy a building—you buy a story. "We saw it before anyone else." "We always wanted something in this suburb." "It reminded me of my grandfather's house." Investors—especially those early in their careers—are often unaware of how quickly stories can become blinders. A derelict cottage with crumbling walls becomes "a charming fixer-upper." A flat with high turnover and problematic tenants is "a hidden gem waiting for the right touch." The danger here is not optimism; optimism has its place. The danger is *identity fusion*—when your self-concept becomes entwined with the asset. Once that happens, every warning signal feels like a personal attack, every suggestion to sell becomes a challenge to your judgement.

The longer an investor clings to a poor decision, the harder it becomes to extract themselves cleanly. Emotional attachment leads to what psychologists call *escalation of commitment*—the compulsion to throw more resources at a failing venture in order to justify earlier actions. A bathroom upgrade here, a new property manager there, a rebranding of the listing—all in the hope that effort will rescue judgment. But as any seasoned investor knows, *effort does not always equal value creation*. Sometimes, the most strategic decision is to absorb the loss, record the lesson, and redeploy your capital and energy elsewhere. Pride, not analysis, is what most often delays this pivot.

Detaching from a property—especially one you've imagined or improved—is not coldness; it's competence. The best investors are not those without emotion, but those who *channel emotion through structure*. They build systems that keep their decision-making rational even when their heart whispers otherwise. One technique is to conduct postmortem analyses before final decisions are made: ask, *If this property underperforms for three more years, what would I wish I had done today?* Another is to involve neutral third parties in your decision loop—people with no stake in your narrative who can interrogate the assumptions you may be protecting subconsciously.

Real-world examples of sunk cost errors are not limited to amateurs. Institutional investors fall into the same traps, albeit on a grander scale. Consider the overcapitalised developments that sit half-empty across parts of suburban Europe—projects greenlit based on political promises or outdated demand forecasts. Despite mounting evidence that demographics had shifted or commuter patterns had changed, developers doubled down. The land was bought, the permits were costly, the renderings were already published. But buildings do not appreciate out of guilt. The market does not care how much you've spent. It only reflects what it's worth now—and what someone is willing to pay.

Equally instructive are the investors who recalibrate quickly. A young investor in Birmingham, after spending £40,000 refurbishing a Victorian terrace to exacting personal standards, listed it for rent at a price the market wouldn't support. Rather than adjust, she held firm for months, believing the right tenant would "see the value." They didn't. After nearly a year of vacancy, she finally accepted a lower rent, but not before losing more in forgone income than she had spent on the upgrades. Her turning point came not through market analysis, but a realisation that *she wasn't investing in property—she was curating a fantasy*. Her recalibration was not just strategic; it was personal growth.

This highlights a deeper truth: *attachment to an idea can be more blinding than attachment to a place.* You may fall in love not with the property itself, but with the idea of being the kind of investor who "sees potential," "has vision," or "proves the doubters wrong." These are ego projects disguised as investment strategies. And they are dangerous, because they invite you to override real-time feedback in favour of a narrative arc. But markets don't reward narrative arcs. They reward agility, timing, discipline—and the humility to admit when something isn't working.

To guard against these traps, sophisticated investors build in deliberate detachment rituals. They review each property's performance as if it were a stock—impersonal, merit-based, unemotional. Some assign an internal benchmark: *Would I buy this again today, at this price, with this data?* Others create quarterly reflection sessions, separating themselves from the day-to-day noise to evaluate portfolio coherence, not just individual asset performance. These practices don't eliminate bias. But they make it visible. And visibility is the first step toward strategic clarity.

Sunk costs and emotional attachments are not weaknesses to be ashamed of—they're inevitable human tendencies. The goal is not to suppress them, but to *design systems that neutralise their power.* That means having an exit plan *before* you fall in love with a deal. It means defining success by actual returns, not effort expended. And it means remembering that *your identity as an investor is not validated by stubbornness—but by adaptability.*

Real estate is not just about accumulating assets. It's about evolving intelligence. And every emotionally-charged mistake, every misread signal, every expensive lesson in detachment has value—*but only if you're willing to learn the right lesson.* Clarity doesn't come from doubling down. It comes from stepping back. When you fall in love with a house or a vision, pause. Ask: *Am I making this decision to protect my ego—or to advance my strategy?* The answer will often determine your outcome.

Chapter 5
Financing Your First Deal Without Losing Your Shirt

If property is the vessel, then finance is the current beneath it. It doesn't simply carry the deal along; it determines whether that vessel floats, drifts off course, or founders altogether. For first-time investors, financing is both lifeline and landmine: a realm where poorly understood decisions compound quietly, and where a fraction of a percentage point, buried in the fine print, can alter the trajectory of an entire portfolio. The myths here are seductive, whispered through glossy seminars, viral reels, and a culture addicted to speed over scrutiny. This chapter is not about "getting the money." It is about understanding money deeply enough that, once borrowed, it does not quietly come to own you.

What most new investors miss is that financing is never a yes-or-no question from a bank. It is a whole ecosystem, shaped by macroeconomics, your credit posture, the quirks of the property itself, lender psychology, and regulatory tides. The interest rate, for instance, is not just a sterile figure on a contract. It is a lens on risk, a measure of global liquidity, a barometer of trust in the wider economy. A rate of 4.5% compared with 5.2% may appear trivial—until you calculate its bite over three decades, when it becomes tens of thousands of pounds. And yet, many first-time buyers put less thought into selecting a mortgage than they do into choosing broadband. That is precisely where danger lies.

At the heart of early investing sits a paradox. You need leverage to start, but leverage is also what makes you most breakable. This chapter does not shy from that tension. We will explore how to employ leverage without turning it into a vanity accelerant—how to frame it instead as scaffolding for durable, long-term growth. Not all deposits are born equal, either. The same 10% down looks very different if it comes from a well-seasoned savings account versus a private arrangement with deferred repayment. Lenders see those sources differently; so should you. Understanding the architecture of your capital stack is every bit as vital as understanding the brickwork it funds.

Then there is credit—that most misunderstood of words. Too often it is reduced to a number, a score pulled from a database. But credit is alive. It is a conversation between your financial history and the world's willingness to back you. Too many novices treat it like an obstacle to be gamed: pay this card off here, tweak that balance there. The more mature perspective sees credit not as a hoop to jump through but as a long-term strategic asset. The goal is not one mortgage approval—it is the creation of enduring access to opportunity. That shift demands moving from score-chasing to reputation-building. We'll unpack how to build, repair, and protect that reputation—long before an application form hits a lender's desk.

We will also examine the less glamorous side of borrowing: the quiet traps embedded in the paperwork. Variable-rate mortgages in volatile cycles, punitive exit clauses hidden inside bridging loans, the intoxicating promise of interest-only terms without any credible repayment plan. Case studies will reveal deals that sparkled on day one, only to unravel under the weight of fine print, skewed incentives, or naïve assumptions about costs and timelines. The conclusion is not that debt is poisonous. Borrowing is amplification. It magnifies discipline into wealth—or magnifies carelessness into insolvency.

Beyond the familiar terrain of bank mortgages lies a wider landscape of funding options. Seller financing, peer-to-peer platforms, private equity partnerships, asset-backed lines of credit. These are not fringe curiosities. They often offer greater flexibility, lower friction, and tighter alignment of interests. Yet they bring complexity, legal nuance, and the need for literacy. A careless handshake with a friend can wreck a deal and a friendship alike; a carefully structured joint venture can launch a career and establish credibility. The difference is not the cash. It is the sophistication.

Too often, financing is treated as an afterthought—an administrative hoop to clear after the property itself has stolen the heart. That is backwards. Finance should shape what you buy, where, when, and how long you intend to hold it. It should determine not just whether the monthly repayment looks manageable, but whether the structure itself is sustainable across cycles. It should inform your views on risk appetite, cash flow resilience, tax strategy, and exit pathways. Financing is not merely fuel. It is part of the engine itself.

Consider the lessons embedded in real stories: a young couple in Manchester who transformed a family gift into a vendor-financed deal that unlocked equity growth conventional lending would never have allowed. A first-timer in London who stretched too far on a variable-rate loan and watched his cash flow collapse within eighteen months. A seasoned investor in Leeds who expanded to eight properties not by saving harder but by understanding mortgage lifecycles and refinancing at the right junctures. These are not tales of luck. They are case studies in financial literacy at work—or absent.

The ambition of this chapter is not to train you to "get approved." It is to train you to think in capital terms, to develop fluency in the grammar of money, time, and risk. Property investment is not only about what you buy. It is about how you capitalise it. That requires sharper questions, precision in place of convenience, and an eye not just on today's yield but tomorrow's solvency. The best investors are not gamblers blessed with charisma. They are architects of structure, designers of durability.

By the close of this chapter, you should be able to interrogate financing rather than merely accept it. You will see the difference between myth and mechanism, learn to spot the traps others miss, and begin to craft your own capital strategies with clarity and confidence. Whether you borrow £40,000 or £400,000, the principle stands: your first deal must build your wealth without breaking your nerve, draining your savings, or crippling your capacity for future moves. That is the standard. Let's begin.

Understanding the Real Cost of Money

There is a strange paradox in property investment: people will agonise over a £5,000 negotiation on the purchase price, yet sign a mortgage agreement that may quietly extract ten times that amount over the course of the loan. The psychology is understandable—purchase price is visible and immediate, whereas interest rates and fee structures are veiled in language few take time to decode. But if you're serious about building wealth through real estate, you cannot afford to be numerically careless. *Small variations in cost, when compounded over time, do not remain small—they shape the financial destiny of the asset.*

A mortgage is not simply a way to acquire a property—it is a contract with time. It governs how money behaves, and therefore how *you* behave. Your repayment structure, interest rate, and fee profile all silently dictate your flexibility, risk tolerance, and profit ceiling. The effective cost of borrowing cannot be reduced to the advertised annual rate or headline term. A 1.5% interest rate on an interest-only product might look superior to a 2.0% on a repayment loan, but the actual long-term implications differ massively once amortisation, inflation, tax treatment, and exit costs are accounted for. *Cheap money isn't always inexpensive money.*

Consider the distinction between fixed-rate and variable-rate loans. A fixed-rate mortgage offers stability—predictable outgoings, easier cash flow modelling, and protection against rate hikes. But that security often comes at a premium, and may include penalties for early repayment or refinancing. A variable-rate loan may start attractively, particularly in low-interest environments, but exposes you to the full force of monetary policy shifts. In a tightening cycle, your payments could climb rapidly, turning a once-sound deal into a monthly liability. *The cost of money is never static—it is a moving organism tied to global economics, national sentiment, and central bank strategy.*

Beyond the rate itself, there's the structure of the loan. Amortisation schedules determine how your equity builds—or doesn't. Interest-only loans may feel like a relief in the short term, but without a disciplined plan for repayment, they often become ticking time bombs. By contrast, loans that front-load interest payments (as many do) give the illusion of progress while actually eroding early-stage equity growth. And then there are balloon payment structures—particularly common in private and development lending—where a significant lump sum is due at the end. Unless you have already secured a clear exit, that lump sum becomes a crisis disguised as a calendar date.

Then there are the silent charges—the hidden costs that lurk in the footnotes. Arrangement fees. Broker commissions. Valuation fees. Legal charges. Early repayment penalties. Exit fees. Redemption penalties. Many borrowers are so fixated on the headline rate that they miss the cumulative burden of these less visible costs. A 0.3% difference in interest might pale in comparison to a £5,000 penalty if you refinance early. *The true cost of capital includes everything you pay to access, service, and exit the debt—not just the rate on the first page.*

A more subtle, and often ignored, aspect of money's cost is *opportunity cost.* By choosing one form of financing over another, you are not merely choosing what you pay—you are determining what options remain available. For instance, if you take a long-term fixed mortgage with restrictive terms, you might be shutting the door to a future refinancing strategy that could unlock equity for a second purchase. Similarly, if you rely on high-interest bridging finance for a flip but the market stalls, you might be forced to sell at a loss just to stop the clock on your lender's compounding fee structure. *Good financing is not just about making the deal work today—it's about keeping the next deal possible tomorrow.*

Let's take a real example. Suppose you purchase a £300,000 property with a 75% loan-to-value mortgage. You're offered two options: one at 3.2% fixed for five years with a £1,000 fee, and one at 2.8% variable with no upfront fee. On paper, the variable looks more appealing. But if interest rates climb by even 1.5% during the term—as they have in recent cycles—you'll pay thousands more in cumulative interest. And if that increase happens to coincide with a major repair, a vacancy, or an unexpected tax liability, you're not just squeezed—you're exposed. Conversely, the fixed-rate might seem expensive, but it offers predictability, which has intrinsic value, particularly in a fragile first investment.

Investors often ask, *What's the best financing option?* That's the wrong question. The right question is: *What is the most appropriate capital structure for the nature of the asset, the state of the market, and the depth of your own risk tolerance?* That may sound complex—but only because we've been trained to treat financing as something we outsource. In truth, understanding your cost of capital is foundational. It is not separate from your strategy. It *is* your strategy.

Another overlooked dimension is tax efficiency. The structure of your mortgage can influence what portion of your interest is deductible, how profits are taxed, and how capital gains are calculated. For example, financing through a limited company structure versus personal ownership carries vastly different implications under UK tax law. Changes in Section 24 of the UK tax code have dramatically altered how landlords can offset mortgage interest—many small investors only realised the impact after seeing their tax bills double. *Finance decisions made without tax awareness are like building on shifting sand.*

Equally important is the sequencing of your financing decisions. Too many first-time investors rush into locking in funds for one deal, only to discover that it constrains their eligibility for future deals. Every borrowing event appears on your credit record, shapes your debt-to-income profile, and adjusts how lenders assess you going forward. The savvy investor plans not just for deal number one, but for deal number two, three, and four. That requires viewing financing as an evolving ecosystem, not a one-time task.

To illustrate, take the case of a pair of early investors in Birmingham who purchased their first buy-to-let using a 90% LTV mortgage with an attractive headline rate. They congratulated themselves on low entry costs, but when the market rose, they were unable to refinance because of restrictive covenants and a lower-than-expected post-renovation valuation. That trapped equity—dead money—forced them to pause for years before scaling. Had they chosen a slightly more expensive product with refinancing flexibility, they could have unlocked their second and third properties within eighteen months. *Cheap entry is meaningless if it costs you strategic mobility.*

There is also a psychological cost to misunderstanding money. Investors who don't grasp how their loans work often fall into reactive behaviours: panic-selling, overcapitalising in renovation, avoiding refinancing even when it's optimal, or underinvesting in maintenance out of fear. On the other hand, those who truly understand their financing terms approach decisions with composure. They are not surprised by rate changes—they anticipate them. They don't chase short-term savings—they optimise long-term positioning.

Finally, the real cost of money is not just monetary—it is *informational.* When you fail to understand how financing works, you become dependent. On brokers, on lenders, on forums filled with half-truths. You lose leverage in negotiations, both with the bank and within your own planning. But when you speak the language of finance fluently, you gain power—because you can see the architecture behind the offer, not just its decoration.

Understanding the real cost of money is not about paranoia. It's about literacy. And that literacy protects you. It allows you to buy better, hold longer, sleep sounder, and scale smarter. It puts you in the mindset of a true investor—not just someone who owns property, but someone who *knows what that ownership actually costs.* That kind of clarity doesn't just preserve wealth. It builds it.

Down Payments Demystified

The down payment has long stood as one of the greatest psychological and financial barriers to entry in real estate investing. It's the lump sum that separates the dreamer from the doer. For most new investors, the concept of a down payment is framed in rigid terms—20% of the property price, paid in cash, sourced from savings. But this conventional wisdom often reflects institutional convenience more than investor necessity. *Not all down payments are created equal, and not all capital has to come from your own pocket.*

Understanding the architecture of a down payment begins with its true function: it is not merely a deposit, but a demonstration of commitment and risk participation. Lenders—whether institutional or private—use it as a filtering mechanism. The more you put in, the more seriously you're presumed to take the investment. But what matters is not the amount per se, but the value and security of the total capital stack. A borrower who offers 10% cash and 10% equity from another property may present less risk than someone offering 20% cash but no fallback assets or experience.

The first step in demystifying the down payment is to strip away the notion that it must be sourced from personal savings. This is a dangerous oversimplification that ignores decades of financial innovation. Seller financing, for example, can significantly reduce or even replace the need for a traditional deposit. If a vendor owns a property outright—or has significant equity—they may be willing to finance part of the deal in exchange for a higher interest rate, faster sale, or income stream. Structuring a down payment as a combination of cash and seller credit can preserve liquidity and create alignment between parties. *The seller becomes your banker, and your negotiation partner—two roles that can be strategically aligned.*

Private lenders—whether individuals, peer-to-peer platforms, or family offices—can also substitute for traditional deposit sources. These arrangements are particularly useful for investors who may be asset-rich but cash-light. Consider a scenario in which an investor owns a property with £100,000 of equity but little free cash. By securing a short-term loan against that equity, they can produce a 25% deposit on a new investment, without selling the original asset. This is leverage with intent: using past success to finance future potential. Of course, it demands discipline and strong cash flow modelling—double leverage is not forgiving of errors. But done correctly, *this strategy turns illiquid equity into entrepreneurial fuel.*

Another underutilised strategy is asset-backed deposits. Many lenders now accept investments, pensions, or even business assets as proof of capital or collateral. For example, a self-invested personal pension (SIPP) may be structured to co-invest in commercial property under certain conditions. Similarly, share portfolios can sometimes be pledged to secure a line of credit that functions as a pseudo-deposit. These techniques require advanced financial literacy, but they unlock doors previously thought closed. *Your down payment does not have to be currency—it can be credibility, collateral, or creativity.*

Let's address the notion of low-deposit schemes offered by the government or financial institutions. Programmes such as Help to

Buy or shared ownership may provide access to property with as little as 5% down. But these schemes come with restrictions—on the type of property, its location, resale terms, or the investor's income bracket. They are not investment tools so much as accessibility mechanisms. That said, for a first-time investor seeking to live in part of the property while renting the other half—a strategy akin to house hacking—these schemes can be leveraged to break the inertia of inaction. *Used judiciously, they provide more than affordability—they provide momentum.*

Crowdfunding and co-investment platforms also offer modern alternatives. By pooling capital with others, investors can gain exposure to property without a traditional down payment. Fractional ownership is rising, particularly in the commercial and short-term rental sectors. While these approaches reduce individual control, they also dilute individual capital requirements. An investor could put £10,000 into five different fractional deals instead of £50,000 into one. This is not merely about affordability—it is about diversification and education. *Your first down payment might buy you a seat at the table rather than the table itself.*

A more advanced technique involves vendor-paid deposits. In distressed sales or developments with cash flow pressures, sellers may agree to fund part of the buyer's deposit by inflating the purchase price and recycling the difference post-completion. While frowned upon by many lenders—and requiring careful legal structuring—this approach has been used effectively in development projects where both parties are sophisticated and transparent. *This is a high-trust, high-risk tool—but in the hands of a seasoned negotiator, it can unlock exceptional deals.*

Case studies bring these principles to life. In Manchester, a young investor acquired a three-unit property valued at £310,000 with just £6,500 of her own money. She secured a bridging loan for 85% of the purchase, negotiated a deferred completion schedule with the seller, and used a private investor to fund the remainder of the deposit in exchange for equity in the rental income. The key wasn't wealth—it was structure, planning, and the ability to explain risk and return clearly to others. This is the new face of property investment: lean on cash, heavy on clarity.

This leads us to a crucial insight: the source of your down payment affects more than your bank balance—it shapes your investor identity. Those who save for years to produce a deposit tend to view the property emotionally—they feel *married* to it. Those who raise capital through partnerships or debt are often more clinical—they see the asset as a vehicle, not a monument. Neither perspective is inherently better, but each produces different decision-making behaviours under stress. *How you acquire is often how you hold.*

Another dimension worth exploring is how down payments intersect with negotiation power. The assumption is that the larger the deposit, the stronger the bargaining position. That is not always true. In hot markets, speed often matters more than size. A buyer with 15% down and a ready bridge loan may outmanoeuvre one with 25% down who needs six weeks to clear bank approval. Similarly, sellers in distress may prioritise certainty over maximum price. Understanding this nuance helps investors deploy their capital where it buys the most influence, not just the most equity. *Cash doesn't always win—but certainty does.*

There is also a cultural myth that bigger deposits are inherently safer. Yes, they reduce loan-to-value ratios and lower borrowing costs. But they also increase exposure. A 30% deposit on a high-risk flip may tie up funds unnecessarily, limiting your ability to pivot if the deal turns. In contrast, a 10% deposit with higher leverage but a strict exit plan may deliver better returns with managed risk. *Risk is not in the leverage—it is in the absence of a plan.*

We must also reckon with the emotional residue of how deposits are perceived. Many investors attach pride to their deposit—especially if it's hard-earned savings. That pride can cloud judgement. They become reluctant to refinance, resistant to joint ventures, or overly conservative in reinvestment. The deposit becomes a symbol of past sacrifice, not future potential. Intelligent investing requires a different lens: viewing capital as a tool, not a trophy. *Your deposit should serve your strategy, not define it.*

Finally, the conversation around down payments must evolve to include *velocity*. That is, how quickly you can redeploy capital. If your deposit remains trapped in a property that appreciates slowly and produces limited cash flow, then it is underperforming. The best investors think not in terms of return on investment (ROI) but return on equity (ROE). They track how long their deposit remains immobilised, and seek ways to refinance, recycle, or reallocate it. This is how professional investors scale: they don't save more—they circulate faster.

To demystify down payments is not to romanticise debt or ignore risk. It is to expand the vocabulary of access. It is to understand that barriers are often illusions reinforced by outdated thinking and rigid formulas. What matters is not how much money you have, but how intelligently you move the money you do have. Whether through creativity, collaboration, or strategy, the modern investor has more options than ever before.

The question, then, is not: *Can I afford a deposit?* The question is: *Can I afford not to understand all the ways a deposit can be designed?* That understanding turns hesitation into action, action into equity, and equity into wealth. And that's how smart investors start—not by waiting, but by learning what the rest of the market assumes.

Mortgages, Loans, and Leverage: A Double-Edged Sword

Leverage is the most powerful accelerant in property investing—and the most misunderstood. It can build a portfolio in half the time or dismantle it in a matter of months. The same instrument that enables an investor to buy five properties instead of one also amplifies every mistake, miscalculation, or market shift. Understanding this duality is essential. To borrow well is not simply to access money—it is to adopt a mindset, a risk discipline, and a long-range framework. *Leverage is not about how much debt you can carry—it's about how much risk you can control.*

At its core, a mortgage is a partnership with a lender. The bank provides the capital, you provide the strategy. But unlike a silent partner in a business venture, your lender cares less about your vision and more about your compliance. They assess affordability, collateral, creditworthiness, and track record. This shapes the boundaries of leverage before a single pound is lent. But here's the truth few new investors understand: *the best leverage isn't found in the mortgage—it's found in the margin.*

Consider two investors. One buys a £300,000 property with a 25% deposit and borrows the remaining £225,000 at 5% interest. The property generates £1,500 per month in rent, and expenses (mortgage, management, maintenance) come to £1,200. That's a modest positive cash flow. The second investor finds a property in a less fashionable postcode, also worth £300,000, but negotiates a vendor discount to buy it at £270,000, and borrows £202,500 on the same terms. Their rent is slightly lower—£1,350—but their costs are proportionately lower too, resulting in greater net income. The second investor's leverage is more efficient, not because they borrowed more or less, but because they borrowed *smarter. Margin control always beats loan size in long-term outcomes.*

A central misunderstanding is the fixation on "how much can I borrow?" instead of "what does this borrowing expose me to?" It is seductive to use high leverage to acquire assets quickly, but high leverage without robust buffers is gambling. Many investors underestimate vacancy periods, maintenance shocks, or interest rate resets. A 1% rate increase on a £250,000 loan is not £2,500—it's £2,500 every year, compounding with every policy cycle. Over a five-year term, that seemingly small difference could erode your profits, force a refinance under duress, or worse—create a cash flow deficit that eats into your personal finances.

Take the example of 2008, when highly leveraged investors in both the UK and the US found themselves overexposed. As property values fell, many were forced into fire sales because they held minimal equity and couldn't refinance. But a quieter group survived—and in many cases thrived—because they managed their leverage proactively. They had lower loan-to-value ratios, fixed interest terms, diversified cash flow streams, and emergency reserves. *They didn't just use debt—they governed it.*

This introduces the idea that leverage is not static. It is fluid and must be managed actively. Interest-only loans, for example, are popular among buy-to-let investors because they reduce monthly outgoings and maximise cash flow. But they defer capital repayment, creating a future liability. If property prices fall or refinancing terms tighten, these investors could find themselves with a shortfall. On the other hand, capital repayment mortgages offer slower portfolio growth but greater long-term stability. The optimal structure depends not on market conditions alone, but on the investor's time horizon, risk appetite, and exit strategy.

The use of leverage must also be calibrated to the investor's stage of development. A first-time buyer with one property and limited reserves should be cautious about over-leveraging. A seasoned investor with ten properties, access to private finance, and strong asset buffers can afford to use more aggressive structures—but even then, within reason. *The more experienced you are, the more conservative you often become—not out of fear, but out of precision.*

Real-world case studies illuminate this. In Birmingham, an investor purchased a five-bed HMO (house in multiple occupation) using a 75% LTV mortgage and a private bridge loan for the refurb. The total leverage exceeded 85%. The cash flow looked strong on paper, but a delayed planning application and a contractor dispute pushed the project beyond budget. With mounting interest costs and no income, the investor was forced to exit at a loss. Contrast that with another investor in Leeds, who purchased a three-bed semi-detached using a 60% LTV mortgage, funded renovations from personal reserves, and refinanced at the new valuation twelve months later—releasing capital but keeping leverage within bounds. The second investor made less upfront, but preserved optionality. *Their leverage was not just cheaper—it was smarter, slower, and ultimately safer.*

Debt reduction strategies should be an integral part of any leverage plan. This includes overpayments, offset mortgages, and equity recycling. Overpayments—making regular or lump sum payments beyond the minimum—can shorten loan terms and reduce total interest exposure significantly. Offset mortgages, which link your savings account to your mortgage balance, reduce interest by treating your savings as a direct deduction on your debt. Equity recycling—refinancing a property after value appreciation to fund the next purchase—requires strict discipline, but when paired with conservative valuations and modest reinvestment, it becomes a tool of sustainable expansion.

There is also a behavioural dimension to leverage. Investors often experience a psychological shift once they become accustomed to using other people's money. They become bolder, more growth-oriented—but sometimes less careful. The line between confidence and hubris is thin. Those who thrive over decades, not just cycles, build in checks. They re-run their numbers under stress test conditions. They assume their interest rates may rise. They account for longer voids. *They prepare for discomfort—not because they expect it, but because they refuse to be blindsided by it.*

Leverage can also distort decision-making in more subtle ways. An investor who has taken on significant debt may feel pressured to hold onto a poorly performing asset simply to avoid crystallising a loss. This is the sunk cost fallacy in financial form. Or they may overvalue gross yields while ignoring net returns, simply to justify the cost of capital. The antidote is to remember that the purpose of leverage is not merely to buy more property—it is to buy *better outcomes.* If the leverage doesn't improve risk-adjusted returns, strengthen liquidity, or expand strategic options, it is not leverage—it is liability.

One final point bears emphasis: your credit profile is not just a gatekeeper to leverage—it is a report card on how you handle financial responsibility. Smart investors cultivate credit not for vanity but for versatility. They monitor their utilisation rates, avoid unnecessary inquiries, and build a history of on-time repayments. This allows them to negotiate better terms, secure funding quickly, and pivot when the market shifts. *Strong credit doesn't guarantee success—but weak credit limits your options before the game begins.*

To wield leverage wisely is to understand it as both science and art. It requires fluency in numbers, sensitivity to cycles, and self-awareness about your own tolerances. It means asking not "what can I afford today?" but "what can I sustain when things don't go to plan?" It is not about buying more aggressively—it is about buying more intelligently. Used correctly, leverage is a force multiplier. Used carelessly, it is a margin call waiting to happen.

The best investors are not those who fear leverage, nor those who glorify it. They are those who *respect* it. They treat debt not as a shortcut to wealth, but as a disciplined tool of expansion—wielded slowly, strategically, and always with an eye on the downside. That respect is what separates speculation from stewardship. And in a world where anyone can borrow, it is discernment—not access—that defines the professional.

Credit as a Tool, Not a Score

It is one of the more persistent misperceptions in personal finance: that your credit score is a fixed badge of identity—like a financial passport that either admits or denies you access to opportunity. But this notion, though widely accepted, is profoundly limiting. A credit score is not an asset in itself. It is not your worthiness as an investor distilled into three digits. Rather, it is a tool—dynamic, interpretable, and, if properly understood, a lever for building long-term access to capital. What matters most is not the number alone, but how you understand the system behind it, how you behave within it, and how strategically you wield it. Those who treat credit as a living financial signal—rather than a judgment handed down—tend to build quietly powerful trajectories through the property world.

Credit, at its core, is behavioural. It reflects probability, not morality. Lenders are not philosophers; they are statisticians. When they assess your credit, they are not deciding whether you are a good person, but whether your past financial decisions offer predictive insight into future performance. Yet for all this objectivity, credit is highly malleable. And therein lies the opportunity: a credit profile can be shaped—sometimes dramatically—through purposeful decisions, sustained habits, and strategic timing. Investors who internalise this principle avoid the common traps of shame, confusion, or passivity. They approach their credit reports like an analyst would approach a company's balance sheet: with curiosity, clarity, and control.

For the first-time property investor, credit is often the first real gatekeeper. It determines whether you are even allowed into the room where financial leverage becomes possible. Many new investors mistakenly assume that if their score is less than pristine, the doors are shut. But the modern lending landscape is far more textured than that. There are traditional banks, yes—but also credit unions, community development lenders, fintech lenders, seller-financed deals, and private investors. Each has a different risk appetite, a different scoring model, and a different timeline. Some weigh credit score heavily; others focus on income consistency, equity in a deal, or even borrower narrative. Understanding this ecosystem is critical if you hope to navigate around short-term limitations or strategically position yourself to access better terms.

Start by recognising what lenders actually see. A credit score is a synthesis of multiple data points: payment history (the single most important factor), credit utilisation, length of credit history, types of credit used, and recent inquiries. But even within this formula, there is nuance. A single missed payment six months ago is weighted differently from one six years ago. Maxing out a credit card in one month is not equivalent to carrying a high balance consistently. Applying for three store cards in a weekend signals something different than refinancing your mortgage. The score is a mathematical outcome, but the report is a narrative. Reading it with care allows you to understand what version of yourself is being presented to lenders.

Now, to credit-building. For the disciplined investor, repairing or elevating credit becomes less about quick fixes and more about architecture. Three principles underpin meaningful credit growth. First: *consistency beats intensity.* A series of on-time payments—even if modest in size—has a cumulative effect far more powerful than a one-off debt clearance. Second: *available credit is more important than used credit.* Keeping your credit utilisation below 30% (ideally below 10%) across all accounts signals responsibility, not neediness. This alone can swing a score dramatically over time. Third: *the age of your accounts matters.* Investors who frequently open and close credit lines—often in pursuit of sign-up bonuses—unknowingly shorten their credit history and destabilise their profile. In contrast, maintaining a few well-aged accounts—even if unused—adds ballast to your financial identity.

There are strategic moves, too, often overlooked by those new to the game. Becoming an authorised user on someone else's long-standing, low-utilisation account can instantly improve your profile—assuming the primary account holder is disciplined. Negotiating with creditors to remove negative entries after a settlement or back-payment can repair not just your balance sheet but your reported history. Using secured credit cards as stepping stones—where your own cash serves as collateral—can re-establish creditworthiness for those starting over. None of these are silver bullets, but in aggregate, they create momentum. And momentum in credit-building is both psychological and numerical. Once you begin to see small score increases, your confidence often returns—and that confidence, paired with continued action, becomes transformative.

Beyond access, credit also impacts *cost*. This is where many property investors fail to fully appreciate its power. A credit score doesn't just determine whether you can borrow, but *on what terms*. A difference of 0.5% in mortgage interest rates—easily triggered by a marginal credit score gap—can result in tens of thousands of pounds in additional payments over a 25-year loan. The same applies to private lender terms, lines of credit, and even insurance premiums. In this sense, improving your credit is not merely about approval—it is about leverage. Better credit translates into cheaper money. And cheaper money multiplies returns, cushions risk, and expands the set of viable deals available to you.

However, this strategic view of credit must always be tempered by ethical clarity. There is a seductive edge to leverage when your credit profile becomes robust. You begin to receive offers: cards, lines, loans, extensions. The disciplined investor evaluates each for its utility, not its flattery. One of the subtler traps in early-stage investing is *overfunding*—accessing more credit than your business model or experience can handle. This is where score obsession becomes dangerous. A 780 credit score is not a licence for reckless expansion. It is a signal that you are trusted. That trust can be used wisely or squandered. And the consequences of misuse—default, foreclosure, insolvency—are punishingly real, especially in property where the stakes are often higher and more public.

We must also acknowledge the structural inequalities embedded in credit systems. Credit reporting, particularly in the United Kingdom and United States, has historically disadvantaged those from low-income backgrounds, immigrants, and individuals without access to traditional financial products. For investors in these categories, the credit path is often steeper. But this makes mastery even more valuable. Understanding how credit functions allows you to advocate for yourself, challenge inaccuracies, and construct alternative paths to legitimacy. Organisations such as Experian Boost and credit unions with flexible underwriting models now provide entry points that were once unavailable. These aren't merely conveniences—they are financial justice tools. Mastery of credit, in this sense, becomes a form of economic agency.

In practical terms, every property investor should treat their credit profile like a balance sheet asset: review it quarterly, protect it aggressively, and improve it intentionally. Before applying for any property-related loan, conduct a full audit. Check for errors. Identify short-term optimisation strategies (e.g., debt pay-downs, removing authorised user accounts with high utilisation). Map out what type of loan product you're seeking—and what credit profile it demands. Then, work backwards to create a credit preparation plan. Done properly, this reduces not just loan rejection risk, but stress, uncertainty, and overexposure.

Ultimately, the serious property investor understands that credit is not about ego or exclusivity. It is about *optionality*. Good credit expands your choices—in lenders, in deals, in timing. And choice, in real estate, is power. Those who can say yes when others can't—and just as critically, say no when others are desperate—operate from a place of strategic advantage. The score, therefore, is just the symptom. What matters most is the underlying signal you send to the financial world: that you are informed, responsible, forward-looking, and quietly prepared. When your credit tells that story, the capital tends to follow.

Chapter 6
What Makes a Good Deal, Really?

Ask ten investors what defines a good deal, and you'll get ten answers—each delivered with conviction, each shaped by personal history, selective memory, and a touch of spreadsheet bravado. Yet beneath the noise sits a quieter truth: "good" is neither fixed nor purely numerical. It is contextual, situational, sometimes even personal. A good deal lives at the crossroads of facts, foresight, and fit. It is less about what the property yields in neat cells on a financial model, and more about how that property aligns with your temperament, your capital, your time horizon, and the life you are, consciously or not, constructing. Numbers matter—of course they do—but they rarely carry the whole tale. The full story is written in neighbourhood undercurrents, timing, capital constraints, discipline, and the evolving self-knowledge of the investor.

This chapter is about sharpening that self-knowledge. Not chasing "cheap" for its own sake, nor following the swirl of headlines and hype cycles, but learning to refine the lens through which you evaluate opportunity. Because opportunity often disguises itself. The best deals are not always the prettiest, or the cheapest, or the ones that appear turnkey. They are the ones that fit—strategically, operationally, philosophically. The investors who repeatedly land such properties are not blessed with luck alone; they see differently. They read beneath the metrics into the deeper story a deal is whispering. This chapter aims to help you hear it too.

To that end, consider the Three-Lens Framework: Numbers, Neighbourhood, Narrative. Not a checklist, but three dimensions that sharpen in relation to one another. Numbers tell you viability: rent-to-price ratio, cash-on-cash returns, holding costs, capex, vacancy exposure. Essential, yes—but insufficient. Neighbourhood brings in the subtler, place-specific signals: schools, tenant mix, local planning quirks, shifting demographics, infrastructure creep. None of these are static; they are currents in motion. And then, the most overlooked lens—Narrative. What role does this deal play in your own arc as an investor? What assumptions are smuggled into your model? Are you chasing cash flow, equity growth, freedom of time—

or some hybrid? It is the narrative that ultimately reveals whether a deal is not just good on paper, but good for you.

Still, even with a framework, reality rarely sits still. Deals seldom arrive in calm clarity. Markets heat up. Emotions rise. Competition warps judgement. Fatigue creeps in. One of the most corrosive forces for beginners is deal desperation—the gnawing urge to buy something, anything, after weeks of missed offers and uninspiring viewings. Standards slip. Numbers are stretched. Location compromises are justified. Rehab costs are shaved down in fantasy. Over time, even bright investors talk themselves into mediocrity just to "get started." The danger here is not ignorance, but impatience. The remedy is not more spreadsheets, but sharper discernment. Seasoned investors are distinguished less by the speed of their "yes" than by the discipline of their "no."

Red flags, predictably, come in many guises. A seller who pushes paperwork too fast. A listing that lingers on the market, yet the price mysteriously holds. A yield propped up only because looming maintenance has been ignored. These warning signs are easy to rationalise away in the heat of momentum. Which is why it pays to approach listings like a forensic reader: to parse estate agent phrasing, to recognise psychological pricing tactics, to distinguish genuine distress from staged urgency. And while scanning for danger, don't overlook the green lights—the quiet positives often hiding in plain sight. A new transport link planned but not yet priced in. An overlooked school catchment with rising reputation. A zone on the cusp of planning reform. Often, the most transformative deals are hiding in the mundane.

Equally important: challenging the reflex that "cheap" equals "good." Many times, the best deal is not the one with the lowest entry price, but the one with the greatest long-term yield in strategic terms. That may mean higher upfront costs but better capital appreciation, stronger tenants, easier refinancing, or a smoother tax profile. This is what I'd call intuitive valuation. Not sloppy guesswork, but layered recognition of value that a spreadsheet alone cannot capture: the loyalty of a tenant base, the growth trajectory of a nearby university, the subtle status shift of a postcode edging upward. These are the human signals that rarely fit into a formula—and yet they often make or break success.

Examples drive the lesson home. A buy-to-let investor who resisted ten supposedly "great" bargains, only to see her patience rewarded when a school rezoning doubled her property's value. A flipper who ignored faint structural hints and paid dearly when subsidence surfaced. A couple who chose to walk from an apparently profitable leasehold because of subtle management issues—saving themselves years of litigation. None of these stories are neat parables. They are reminders that property is not just an asset class, but an operating commitment. Every purchase ties you to a mesh of obligations, dependencies, and trajectories. Misjudge the fit, and you inherit not just poor yield but compounding hassle.

So, rather than offer universal formulas or paint-by-numbers checklists, this chapter lays out a way of thinking: a flexible, disciplined system that integrates metrics with place, and place with personal alignment. Yes, you'll leave with tools for due diligence. But more importantly, you'll leave with a keener sense of your own criteria. For in real estate, clarity is a competitive advantage. The sharper your definition of a "good deal," the more confidently you can negotiate, decline, or act decisively when the right one appears.

At bottom, this chapter is about elevation. A shift from reacting to whatever crosses your inbox, hoping to stumble into a bargain, to a proactive stance: weighing each opportunity through lenses of financial rigour, spatial intelligence, and personal fit. The goal isn't merely to find a good deal. It's to know precisely why it's good—and to have the composure to walk, wait, or seize it when the moment comes.

The Three-Lens Framework: Numbers, Neighbourhood, Narrative

Ask an experienced investor why they passed on a property that looked profitable on paper, and they'll likely give you an answer that sounds deeply intuitive, even personal. "It just didn't feel right." On the surface, such responses may seem at odds with the rational world of investment metrics. But behind these instincts is usually a rigorous mental model—one shaped by experience and grounded in a framework far more nuanced than spreadsheets alone. That framework, in its most complete form, rests on three interdependent pillars: numbers, neighbourhood, and narrative. Each lens sharpens a different dimension of a potential deal. Overlooking even one often leads to outcomes that look efficient but prove unsustainable.

The first lens—*numbers*—is, of course, essential. A deal that doesn't make financial sense isn't worth pursuing, no matter how attractive the postcode or how compelling the backstory. But too often, novice investors fall into the trap of treating numbers as the only lens. The model becomes dangerously reductionist: yield equals merit; cash-on-cash return is king. What this misses is context. Numbers without story are brittle. They can be manipulated, misread, or disconnected from real-world drivers like tenant demand, market liquidity, and neighbourhood trajectory. A spreadsheet is only as useful as the assumptions behind it, and if those assumptions don't account for what's happening on the ground or inside the property, they're not projections—they're delusions.

That's where the *neighbourhood* lens comes in. Properties are not abstract assets; they're stitched into social, geographic, and economic ecosystems. A flat in a rapidly gentrifying area carries different risks and opportunities from a bungalow in a stagnant suburb—even if both generate identical rental yields today. Understanding neighbourhoods means examining zoning laws, school districts, transit plans, demographic shifts, crime trends, and the pace of development. It means walking the streets, not just Googling them. A number-cruncher may see two postcodes with similar cap rates and conclude they're interchangeable. A sophisticated investor knows that one may be on the brink of appreciation while the other teeters toward decline. Importantly, *this lens must also include what cannot be neatly quantified*—reputation, cultural fit, and a sense of whether the area aligns with your values and vision as a property owner.

But the most underappreciated—and most quietly powerful—lens is *narrative*. Every investment carries a story: of how it came to be, who lives there, and what role it will play in your portfolio. Narrative is not about sentimentalism. It's about alignment. Does this property support your long-term goals, or does it create noise and distraction? A cash-rich investor approaching retirement might seek stable, low-maintenance income in a town they know intimately. A young professional with a high-risk appetite may look to convert undervalued assets in emerging markets. These investors aren't choosing different assets by accident; they're choosing different narratives that map to their own identity, risk tolerance, and lifestyle. And the most seasoned investors are honest with themselves about the stories they're buying into—whether it's a calculated repositioning or a vanity play masquerading as a "value-add."

To illustrate the value of this tripartite model, consider the case of a Victorian terrace in East Manchester. The numbers looked impeccable: an 8.2% gross yield, projected capital appreciation of 5% annually, and tenants already in situ. On paper, a near-perfect acquisition. But a walk through the surrounding area revealed a different story: vacant storefronts, inconsistent rubbish collection, and a pending council proposal to re-zone adjacent blocks for light industrial use. Speaking with locals added more colour: antisocial behaviour had spiked in the previous 18 months, and tenant turnover had risen sharply. The investor ultimately passed. Not because the numbers lied, but because the neighbourhood narrative didn't align with the stability goal of their existing portfolio. The same deal might have made sense for someone with a short-term flipping strategy, but it was misaligned with this investor's broader arc.

By contrast, a more expensive but seemingly "overpriced" flat in a seaside town undergoing regeneration was purchased, despite a mediocre initial yield. Why? Because the investor's research into local infrastructure upgrades—backed by government incentives and private sector investment—suggested long-term uplift. The property aligned with their narrative of building intergenerational wealth through legacy locations, not quick wins. Over the next five years, the flat outperformed many higher-yielding assets bought by peers in "better" statistical areas. That investor wasn't lucky—they were looking through all three lenses.

Of course, tension between these lenses is inevitable. A property may offer stellar returns (numbers) but lie in a neighbourhood that clashes with your long-term strategy or tenant base (neighbourhood), or it may fit your desired narrative but require overpaying in a hot market. The strength of the framework lies not in eliminating trade-offs but in making them explicit. It surfaces conflicts early and demands clarity: What are you optimising for? Where are you willing to compromise? And what does that reveal about the investor you are becoming?

There's also an ethical dimension worth surfacing. Investors who view deals solely through the financial lens may overlook—or even perpetuate—harmful dynamics: tenant displacement, neglect of community needs, and transactional landlord-tenant relationships. But when neighbourhood and narrative enter the equation, a richer picture emerges—one that can integrate financial performance with social awareness and long-term stewardship. *Good investment does not mean predatory investment.* It means clarity about impact as well as return.

Critically, the three-lens model is not static. As your portfolio matures, so too should your evaluative depth. In the early stages, you may lean heavily on numbers to stay solvent. Over time, narrative and neighbourhood can take precedence, helping you shape a portfolio that is not only profitable but coherent. Some investors find themselves recalibrating completely: selling high-yield units that no longer serve their lifestyle goals, or exiting gentrifying neighbourhoods where tenant relationships have become adversarial. This is evolution, not failure. It's a sign that your strategy is adapting to deeper truths about your temperament, your purpose, and your priorities.

To treat property as merely transactional is to miss its profound complexity. A successful deal is not merely one that cash flows on day one. It is one that holds up to scrutiny across all three lenses—financial viability, community intelligence, and personal resonance. This framework does not guarantee profit. What it offers is something rarer: alignment. And from alignment comes resilience—the kind that carries investors not only through market cycles, but through the inevitable changes in their own ambitions and convictions.

Approach every potential acquisition, then, not with tunnel vision but with triple vision. Numbers tell you if a deal can work. Neighbourhood reveals where it will work. Narrative explains why it should matter to you at all. Ignore any one of these, and you risk investing with half a mind. Embrace all three, and you begin investing with your whole intelligence.

Red Flags and Green Lights:

Every seasoned investor develops a kind of second sight—not mystical, but hard-earned. It's the ability to read between the lines of a listing, to spot what's missing rather than what's highlighted, and to sense when a seller's urgency smells more like pressure than opportunity. This isn't about paranoia or overanalysis. It's about learning to observe patterns that others overlook, which, over time, can mark the difference between building equity and buying regret.

The modern property market rewards speed, but punishes haste. Platforms promise one-click viewing requests, bidding wars erupt within hours of listing, and emotionally charged language often clouds otherwise mediocre assets. Amid this noise, the disciplined investor must do something deeply unfashionable: pause. That pause is where red flags emerge—not through suspicion, but through structured attentiveness.

Consider the language of the listing. Terms like "cosy" may obscure cramped layouts; "character" might mask outdated infrastructure. "Sold as-is" is rarely a blank canvas—it's a warning that the vendor is disengaging from responsibility. But these red flags aren't absolute deal-killers. The art lies in deciphering whether a warning is a symptom of deeper dysfunction or merely a negotiable inconvenience. A property that needs rewiring isn't a disaster if the price anticipates it. But if the asking price rivals turnkey homes nearby, that's a mismatch no spreadsheet can justify.

Seller behaviour offers its own set of clues. A seller who reschedules viewings repeatedly may be disorganised—or may be hiding something. Sellers who linger during tours, adding commentary to every room, often seek to distract or emotionally influence. Equally, sellers who withhold standard documentation—structural surveys, tenant history, planning permissions—are not merely disorganised. They're betting on a buyer who won't ask twice. *Professionalism—or the lack thereof—tends to be contagious; deal with disorder now, and it may follow you into ownership.*

Market data, too, can be both a map and a minefield. If a property has been relisted multiple times over a year with minimal price adjustment, ask why. Properties that stagnate tend to do so for structural reasons: poor access, flood risk, title issues. Conversely, a sharp price drop within a fortnight of listing is less likely to be generosity and more likely to mask an urgent exit—financial stress, legal deadline, or worse. Either way, data points must be read not as standalone facts but as signals in a behavioural system.

But not every cautionary sign is a cause to walk away. The discipline of investing lies as much in noticing green lights—hidden value—as in flagging risks. A poorly staged flat in a well-performing school catchment may have untapped rental appeal. A house with outdated interiors but sound roofing and double glazing might simply suffer from aesthetic neglect. What looks like a distressed asset to a novice might represent sweat equity to an experienced eye. The key is developing pattern recognition: *where others see hassle, the trained investor sees margin.*

Take the example of a two-bedroom semi-detached in a tertiary city, sitting unsold for six months due to garish paint and poor photos. Surface flaws, yes—but a closer review of the land registry revealed it had been in the same ownership for three decades, suggesting minimal mortgage leverage. A quiet enquiry unearthed a motivated seller facing retirement abroad. The investor who bought it did so 7% under asking, redecorated with minimal capital, and rented it to a local professional couple within a fortnight of completion. This wasn't luck—it was clarity, grounded in the ability to filter signal from noise.

What enables such discernment is a structured approach to analysis—one that extends beyond instinct but still includes it. Red flags often cluster. Rarely does a problematic property signal concern in just one domain. You might find opaque tenancy arrangements, absent building regulation approvals, and unresolved boundary disputes coexisting. The novice tries to fix these in isolation; the experienced investor sees the pattern and walks away. Likewise, green lights rarely stand alone. A property located near future infrastructure upgrades, priced modestly, with stable rental history, and modest repair needs—that's not a fluke. It's a convergence. You earn the right to act on it through due diligence.

This is where the discipline of building and using a visual checklist proves transformative. Not a formula, but a rigorous habit. The best investors develop scorecards that account for both qualitative and quantitative insights: not just rental yield, but also neighbourhood trajectory, maintenance history, tenant churn, zoning shifts, and macroeconomic tailwinds. Over time, these checklists become embedded thinking—not boxes to tick, but filters to apply intuitively. And intuition, as any disciplined thinker knows, is often memory disguised as speed.

It's also worth recognising the emotional component. *Red flags often whisper, green lights rarely shout.* Our brains are primed to notice urgency and fear more than subtler signals of value. This cognitive asymmetry can lead investors to overcorrect—fleeing at the first sign of ambiguity while failing to recognise upside hiding in plain sight. Emotional discipline means learning to test a red flag rather than panic, and to verify a green light rather than celebrate prematurely.

The market itself can amplify confusion. In rising markets, almost everything looks like a green light. Complacency sets in; due diligence becomes optional. In down markets, red flags proliferate—some valid, some not—and hesitation becomes chronic. A wise investor develops filters that hold across both climates. If a deal only makes sense in a boom, it's not a good deal. If it holds under scrutiny in a downturn, it's likely worth serious attention.

Ultimately, the discipline of reading red flags and green lights isn't just about risk management—it's about decision clarity. Every property represents a bundle of signals, and every decision reflects the investor's ability to interpret those signals without distortion. *Success isn't about never making mistakes; it's about learning to see the avoidable ones before they compound.* As with all forms of pattern recognition, the quality of perception is earned—not gifted—and shaped by deliberate reflection, structured analysis, and the courage to walk away from the almost-right.

And that is the most underrated green light of all: the sense of calm that comes not from landing the deal, but from knowing why you said yes—or no—with full awareness.

Deal Fatigue and Desperation:

Most property investors don't fail because they lack knowledge. They fail because, somewhere between the 23rd and 41st viewing, they lose patience. Deal fatigue sets in—quietly at first, then all at once. The discipline that once guided decisions starts to erode under the weight of exhaustion, and the once-clear investment strategy bends under emotional strain. The spreadsheet still runs the numbers, but the mind, weary of uncertainty, begins negotiating with itself: *'Maybe this one is good enough. Maybe perfect is the enemy of done."* And so, the investor makes the most expensive compromise of all—settling.

Fatigue-driven decisions are rarely obvious in the moment. They wear the mask of practicality. Investors tell themselves they're adapting to market conditions, or that the opportunity cost of waiting is too high. But what often hides beneath this surface logic is desperation—the emotional friction between strategic patience and psychological closure. *After months of searching, a mediocre deal can begin to look like a rescue boat. The danger is mistaking temporary discomfort for structural urgency.*

At the core of deal fatigue is an identity conflict. New investors often start with a crisp, well-reasoned thesis: a target yield, an ideal location, a risk profile they can live with. But as weeks stretch into months, that strategy begins to feel like a burden. The investor isn't just hunting for a property—they're wrestling with self-doubt. *If everyone else is buying, what am I missing? If nothing fits my criteria, is the problem the market—or me?* These are not merely intellectual questions. They reflect a deeper human tendency: when the world doesn't mirror our expectations, we often adjust our expectations before questioning the mirror.

Desperation tends to distort in two key ways: first, it narrows perception; second, it inflates justification. When you're tired of looking, you begin to see what you want to see—and ignore what you don't. A leaky roof becomes "manageable with insurance." A weak rental market becomes "an opportunity to test demand." You become generous in your assumptions, creative in your risk framing, and tolerant of flaws you once dismissed out of hand. And because your brain craves a resolution, it rewards you with a temporary hit of relief when you lower your standards. *But relief is not return. Closure is not profit.*

The solution is not to power through with more effort, but to recalibrate your expectations of the process itself. *Every serious investor must normalise rejection as part of the craft.* Saying "no" 39 times isn't a failure; it's pattern recognition in action. Reframing the search from "finding a deal" to "eliminating poor candidates" reduces psychological friction. It shifts you from a deficit mindset to a filter mindset—where every unsuitable viewing confirms that your standards still hold, rather than suggesting you're being too picky.

There is also a practical benefit to structured discipline: it builds compounding clarity. Each deal you turn down should sharpen your internal compass. What once felt like preference becomes principle. Maybe you thought you were open to multiple cities, but after 20 viewings, you realise the rental dynamics in one of them are too opaque for your risk tolerance. Maybe you thought a 5% yield was your baseline—but after six meetings with letting agents, you learn the void risk in that region erodes effective income. These are not failures; they are data. But they only become insight when processed from a place of composure, not frustration.

Resisting desperation also requires systemic guardrails—pre-committed constraints that protect your judgement when your emotional energy dips. This could be a checklist you must complete before any offer is submitted, a mandatory 48-hour cool-off period before negotiating terms, or a requirement to have a second investor or advisor review your deal logic. *Self-discipline is rarely enough in the moment; the most effective investors outsource discipline to process.*

A revealing case study comes from a London-based professional who spent over a year looking for a rental property in Birmingham. After dozens of showings, rising interest rates, and a few near-miss bids, she finally purchased a two-bed flat with below-market rent and a short lease. She justified the choice with vague hopes of renegotiating lease terms and "potential" future appreciation. A year later, the lease extension proved costlier than expected, void periods lingered, and yield fell far below projections. When asked what changed her mind about the deal, her response was telling: *"I was just so tired of looking."* The price of that fatigue wasn't just financial—it was reputational. It delayed her portfolio growth, dented her confidence, and disrupted the clear-headed logic she once prided herself on.

By contrast, another investor working the same region took a break after 35 viewings. He stepped back, re-reviewed his initial thesis, and adjusted his criteria—not by lowering standards, but by clarifying constraints. He realised that his stress came not from the properties, but from uncertainty about his financing options. With a restructured financing plan, he resumed his search four months later and secured a small HMO that exceeded his original yield target. *His discipline wasn't about waiting—it was about knowing what not to compromise.*

Deal fatigue thrives in environments where goals are vague and strategy is reactive. To prevent emotional erosion, investors must have clarity not only on what they want, but also on what they will not accept. This is the difference between outcome obsession and process integrity. The latter allows you to make slow, confident progress—even through frustration—because your sense of success isn't tied to the next offer. It's grounded in alignment.

Finally, it's crucial to recognise the long arc of a property career. One deal is never final. A good decision today sets the conditions for better decisions tomorrow. A rushed decision today sets the conditions for recovery tomorrow. *The real cost of settling isn't just the underperformance of that one property; it's the inertia, regret, and risk-aversion it seeds into your future thinking.*

Patience isn't just a virtue in real estate—it's a competitive advantage. In a market where others cave to pressure, your ability to stay strategically still becomes an act of strength. And when the right deal finally does appear—one that meets your financial, structural, and strategic criteria—you'll be able to recognise it with full conviction, not because it ends the search, but because it fulfils the purpose. That clarity, earned through restraint, is what distinguishes a reactive buyer from a deliberate investor.

When the Best Deal Isn't a Bargain:

The most expensive mistake a property investor can make is assuming that a low price equals a good deal. Beneath that surface-level thinking lies a dangerous illusion—that value is synonymous with discount. But the most sophisticated investors understand that value and price are not the same currency. In fact, many of the highest-performing assets in a property portfolio don't begin as bargains; they begin as properties others overlook because the asking price appears too ambitious or the yield too modest. What separates the seasoned investor from the opportunistic buyer is the ability to see beyond the spreadsheet—to intuit, model, and strategically assess *why* a higher-priced asset might actually deliver disproportionate returns in the long run.

Value is multi-dimensional, and price-per-square-foot is among its most primitive measures. A property's headline cost tells you little about future demand, the quality of tenants it will attract, its capital appreciation trajectory, or the stability of its surrounding infrastructure. This is especially true in neighbourhoods undergoing regeneration or cultural revaluation—areas where early signals of growth haven't yet filtered into asking prices. In these contexts, price lags behind value. The ability to detect and invest during that lag is what distinguishes market watchers from market movers.

Consider a two-bed flat in a central zone of Manchester's Northern Quarter listed at £285,000—10% above local comparables. At first glance, it seems overpriced. But on closer inspection, it's in a boutique block with no cladding concerns, direct tram access, and service charges that are 40% lower than nearby new builds. It also borders a fast-emerging co-working and lifestyle cluster. The immediate yield may not thrill the spreadsheet, but its five-year capital appreciation, tenant stability, and rent elasticity make it far more valuable than a cheaper flat five streets away with higher void risk and future remediation costs. *The best deal isn't the one with the lowest sticker—it's the one with the highest multidimensional value curve.*

This kind of valuation demands a broader lens—one that incorporates time horizon, tenant demographics, infrastructure development, and your personal or institutional strategy. A higher-priced property in a stable school catchment with low crime rates and strong transport links may feel expensive today but protect you from churn, arrears, and volatility later. *It is a hedge against headaches, not just inflation.*

There's also an under-discussed behavioural dimension to value: how the property fits into your life, temperament, and ambitions. Investors often underestimate the psychological cost of managing underperforming assets. A "cheap" deal that ends up draining your time, peace of mind, and liquidity is no deal at all. Conversely, a higher-priced property that aligns with your preferred style of ownership—low-maintenance, strong governance, reliable tenants—can amplify not only your returns but your staying power in the game. *A wise investor doesn't just optimise for numbers; they optimise for longevity.*

Let's examine a contrasting pair of London-based investments from 2016. One investor acquired a two-bed flat in Barking for £250,000—a price well below London's average. The projected yield was strong, but the building was poorly managed, tenant turnover was high, and the promised Crossrail uplift took years to materialise. Six years on, growth stalled and multiple remedial works emerged. Another investor paid £420,000 for a compact flat in a fully refurbished Victorian block in Finsbury Park—arguably overpriced on paper. But the tenant profile was resilient, voids were rare, and capital appreciation surged in tandem with a rising local amenities scene. By 2022, the "expensive" flat outperformed not just in value but in time saved, stress avoided, and reputational risk managed. *The numbers tell one story; lived experience tells the full one.*

Much of this insight boils down to resisting the allure of price-based heuristics. Humans are hardwired to feel smart when negotiating a lower price. But intelligent investing isn't about scoring discounts—it's about allocating capital to assets that reward you asymmetrically over time. This means expanding your due diligence beyond the conventional checklist and incorporating what might be termed intuitive valuation. That includes asking:

Who will want this property five, ten, or fifteen years from now?

What structural, demographic, or economic tailwinds support this asset?

What reputational, regulatory, or maintenance risks are not reflected in the asking price?

How does this asset perform under stress—interest rate hikes, market dips, or policy shifts?

Intuitive valuation doesn't mean guessing. It means synthesising quantitative and qualitative data into a narrative you can invest in. It's what allows you to pay above average and still walk away with a better-than-average result—because you're solving for resilience, adaptability, and future demand, not just a margin on purchase.

There is, of course, a danger in over-rationalising high prices. Not every premium listing is secretly undervalued. But that's where discipline and comparative analysis come into play. The key isn't to always buy high—it's to buy high *when the market has mispriced long-term value.* And the only way to recognise such mispricing is to have a clear, repeatable framework for how you assess value creation beyond the purchase date.

Part of that framework involves thinking in terms of utility. What is the asset going to do for you—not just this year, but next decade? Does it offer optionality: the ability to convert, refinance, redevelop, or exit flexibly? Does it give you access to markets or tenant groups that other assets cannot? These questions rarely show up in a conventional valuation report, yet they often determine whether a property becomes a strategic asset or a stranded cost.

One useful thought experiment is to ask: if this property were a business, would I want to own it? Investors instinctively scrutinise operational risk, brand durability, and customer lifetime value when assessing companies. Yet many ignore these lenses in property—treating houses as static objects rather than active, service-producing investments. But property, like any enterprise, has inputs (maintenance, management), outputs (income, appreciation), and market-facing dynamics (location, legislation, competition). When a property scores well across these fronts, paying a premium is not reckless—it's rational.

A final note: the market often punishes short-term frugality with long-term drag. Buying the cheapest unit in a block with weak management can cost more in repairs, disputes, and tenant problems than a pricier unit in a well-run freehold. Equally, a below-market price in a marginal location can lock you out of appreciation cycles and limit refinancing potential. The real return, in many cases, comes not from the deal you struck on Day One but from the stability and opportunities that asset enables over the next 3,650 days.

The most powerful investors are those who understand this distinction and act accordingly. They don't chase bargains—they hunt value. They calibrate their vision not by what's on sale, but by what will endure. And in doing so, they free themselves from the tyranny of the discount and embrace the discipline of discernment.

Chapter 7
Making Your Money Work—Cash Flow and Tax Plays

No matter how elegant the theory behind your property strategy, it must eventually face the bluntest of interrogations: does the money actually work? Real estate, with its timelines stretching across decades and its decisions compounding in unexpected ways, is ruthless in this respect. What distinguishes the seasoned from the naïve is not vision alone, but the practical art of making money behave. Yes, cash flow matters—it keeps the lights on and cushions the shocks—but to pursue it blindly is to court distortion. The wiser truth is that cash flow, tax design, and net returns operate as an interlocking system. Pull one lever without understanding the others, and the machine misfires. Most new investors never quite grasp that.

Property is a game of margins, certainly, but it is also a game of interpretation. Many losses arise not because the arithmetic was sloppy, but because the meaning of the numbers was misread. A rental may show a pleasant surplus on a spreadsheet, but has inflation been accounted for? The inevitable vacancy gaps? Or the capital expenditure bombs waiting in year three, five, or seven, when roofs, boilers, and wiring conspire to demand six figures? Too often, spreadsheets behave like stage sets: tidy façades concealing the mess backstage. The aim of this chapter is to prise open those shadows—to reveal the soft costs, the hidden risks, and the subtle advantages that live between the cells.

We begin, naturally, with cash flow. All too often it is treated as the sole arbiter of deal quality—as though the monthly surplus were a definitive grade. But that narrow view ignores its true role: not just income, but buffer; not just surplus, but signal. Cash flow under pressure reveals more about your portfolio's resilience than it does in times of calm. For some, it is indispensable—those who rely on rental income to sustain daily living must guard it fiercely. For others, whose eyes are fixed on long-term equity growth, short-term deficits may be acceptable if appreciation, leverage, and tax structure work in concert. The art lies in knowing which camp you belong to—and when your priorities must shift.

From here we tread into territory most prefer to ignore: taxes. They are too often treated as a postscript, a nuisance to be endured once the deal is inked. Yet in truth, tax structures are levers of immense power, capable of transfiguring pedestrian returns into excellent ones. This chapter does not deal in secret tricks or dubious loopholes. It deals in clarity. We examine depreciation, capital gains frameworks, and the reinvestment vehicles that vary by jurisdiction—1031 exchanges in the United States, rollover relief in the United Kingdom, cost-base resets in Australia. Experienced investors use these not as afterthoughts but as cornerstones of design, building portfolios with tax as architecture, not as patchwork.

Still, no elegance of tax planning can resuscitate an asset that leaks unseen. Vacancy, repair shocks, inflation erosion—these are the slow killers. They do not announce themselves in glossy brochures. They arrive gradually, through rent not collected, emergency call-outs at midnight, or operational costs rising stealthily against static income. To construct an honest model of profit, you must budget for impermanence as deliberately as you do for mortgage repayments. This is less pessimism than realism.

And then, we widen the aperture. Property, unlike equities, is anchored in place—but its context is increasingly global. Taxation regimes, incentives, and holding benefits differ markedly between nations, and understanding those contrasts is no mere academic exercise. Whether you plan to invest abroad, relocate, or simply anticipate domestic reforms, learning how jurisdictions treat depreciation, capital gains, and rental income arms you with a strategist's perspective. The most successful investors of this era are not only precise analysts of local deals, but interpreters of cross-border complexity.

Threading through all of this is a unifying idea: profit is not a static number but a living process. It breathes with cash flow, tax leverage, market risk, and the erosions we prefer not to admit. Treat these elements dynamically and you cease being a hobbyist; you become a strategist. You stop seeing properties as prices to be paid, and start seeing them as financial organisms—shaped by law, economics, tenants, and your own aims.

The lesson is not a neat formula but a shift in stance. Properties that make your money truly work are not always the ones that appear cheapest or most cash-rich at first glance. They are the ones that, over years, align with your liquidity needs, your tax context, and your appetite for uncertainty. That alignment does not happen by chance. It must be designed—consciously, with discipline, and with every available tool.

By the close of this chapter, it should be clear: successful investors are not merely adept with numbers. They are deft with nuance. They know that real wealth in real estate does not spring from chasing rents or shaving taxes, but from orchestrating the whole system—cash, law, market, psychology—towards a defined endgame.

Why Cash Flow Isn't Everything (But Still Matters)

Ask a room full of real estate investors what defines a "good deal," and most will answer reflexively: *positive cash flow.* The phrase has become a mantra, a safety signal, and a shorthand for financial sanity. And to be clear, it's not wrong. Cash flow—the surplus income left after all expenses are paid—is one of the most important indicators of a property's resilience and utility. It keeps the lights on, the mortgage covered, and your stress levels down. But treating cash flow as the sole arbiter of investment quality is reductive, even hazardous. *The fixation on monthly surplus can distract you from broader strategic value—or lull you into a false sense of security.*

This article challenges the oversimplification of cash flow as either a box to tick or a fixed benchmark. It examines cash flow's true function as a *risk management tool, a reinvestment engine, and a lifestyle enabler*—but also explains when it may not be the right primary focus. We will look at situations where negative or minimal cash flow is acceptable, even desirable, and when it represents a ticking bomb. As with most things in investing, context is king. Numbers don't operate in a vacuum—they operate within your goals, your capital constraints, and your long-range plan. *Cash flow matters. But it matters differently depending on what you're trying to build.*

At its most basic, cash flow refers to the net income generated by a property after all operating expenses, taxes, maintenance, insurance, management fees, and mortgage payments are accounted for. That leftover sum—often modest on single-family homes or starter flats—is what many investors chase. But what's often missed is that *cash flow is not profit*. It's not ROI. It's not even true yield. It is *liquidity*, not necessarily wealth. Cash flow provides buffer, flexibility, and some margin for error. But it does not automatically imply that an investment is appreciating, or that the capital is being used in its highest and best form.

Why, then, has cash flow become so central in the real estate lexicon? In part because it is tangible. You can see it arrive in your account each month. It reassures you that the asset is "doing something." For those pursuing financial independence or early retirement, monthly cash flow represents freedom: income that is detached from employment. And for highly leveraged investors, positive cash flow provides a protective shield against rising interest rates or tenant delinquency. *Viewed in this light, cash flow is less about growth and more about defence.* It protects your downside and ensures you are not forced to sell in a distressed market.

However, the real estate landscape varies dramatically depending on geography, market cycle, and investment type. In high-growth urban centres like London, Toronto, or Sydney, cash flow is often negative in the early years—yet the capital appreciation can be substantial. Investors in these environments might endure years of out-of-pocket subsidy, betting on a large equity payoff. This is not irrational. It is a calculated risk, rooted in long-term vision. But it requires *sophisticated planning and deep financial reserves*. It's a luxury not afforded to all.

Contrast this with tertiary markets in the American Midwest or parts of Eastern Europe, where entry prices are low and rental yields are high. There, cash flow is easy to generate—but the risk lies in stagnation. Capital values may remain flat for a decade. Tenant quality may be volatile. Appreciation, if it comes, is often inflation-driven rather than fundamentals-based. The cash looks good on paper, but the long-term wealth-building potential can be limited. *An investor who understands this tension is more likely to choose assets that align with their real goals—not just their spreadsheets.*

There is also a psychological layer. Cash flow soothes anxiety. It reassures investors that they have "bought well." But this comfort can mask complacency. Properties that yield consistent but modest returns often delay tougher strategic questions: Is this asset worth holding for 10 years? Could that equity be deployed elsewhere more aggressively? What are the tax implications of holding versus selling? These questions are uncomfortable—but essential. *A surplus of £200 a month might feel like victory, but if the capital appreciation is zero and your opportunity cost is high, it may be false comfort.*

On the flip side, ignoring cash flow entirely is often the mistake of the overconfident. Some investors, especially those coming from equity markets, buy real estate with the assumption that it will act like a growth stock—producing no yield but appreciating spectacularly. This thinking collapses the moment market cycles turn. Illiquidity, vacancies, or rising interest costs can crush underperforming properties. Without cash flow, your holding power diminishes. *Cash flow doesn't make you rich—but the absence of it can make you poor quickly.*

Cash flow also plays a critical role in *reinvestment velocity*—your ability to scale. If your property portfolio is entirely equity-rich but cash-flow poor, you may struggle to extract capital for new deals. On the other hand, modest but reliable cash flow allows you to build reserves, qualify for loans, and seize time-sensitive opportunities. It gives you optionality. You can choose to reinvest, upgrade, or simply pause without panic. For those pursuing portfolio expansion, cash flow serves as a *compounding catalyst.*

Where cash flow becomes especially powerful is when integrated into a broader risk management framework. Say you are holding five properties across different markets. One may be equity-heavy but cash-light. Another may be cash-rich but exposed to local economic downturns. A balanced portfolio doesn't rely on any single property for liquidity or upside. Instead, it *layers risk across time horizons and cash-flow profiles.* This allows you to sustain through lean cycles and capitalise during booms.

There's also a tax dimension. In many jurisdictions, positive cash flow is taxed more heavily than unrealised capital gains. For investors in higher brackets, generating substantial monthly cash flow can create unintended tax drag. Strategic investors account for this. They may use cost segregation, depreciation, or interest deductions to shield income. Others may intentionally structure their holdings to produce low-to-moderate cash flow while prioritising equity build-up. *There is no one-size-fits-all strategy—only alignment between what the property offers and what you need it to do.*

One final point often overlooked: cash flow is not guaranteed. Maintenance costs spike. Property taxes rise. A tenant vacates unexpectedly. A new rent control ordinance passes. All of these can erode cash flow within weeks. Investors who rely on best-case scenarios—who assume that last year's numbers will hold steady—are often caught off-guard. *Sustainable cash flow must be tested against stress scenarios.* What happens if your rent drops by 10%? What if your mortgage resets at a higher rate? What if inflation outpaces your rent increases? Modelling downside scenarios is not pessimism; it's prudence.

Ultimately, the goal is to graduate from binary thinking—"positive cash flow good, negative bad"—into strategic thinking. Ask: *What role does cash flow play in my broader financial picture?* Am I using it as income? As liquidity? As leverage? Or simply as psychological reassurance? Then adjust accordingly. Some properties should pay you monthly. Others should quietly grow your net worth. A few rare ones will do both. But you must *know which is which—and why you're holding them.*

This is why cash flow matters. But not in the simplistic way most would have you believe. It matters as part of a whole—integrated with appreciation, tax treatment, liquidity goals, and market risk. Treated wisely, it's not just a number on a spreadsheet. It's *a signal—of health, of discipline, and of foresight.* And understanding how and when to listen to that signal may be the difference between a portfolio that survives, and one that truly thrives.

Taxes as Strategy, Not Burden

Most investors treat taxes as something to be endured. A necessary evil. An afterthought added once the deal is done and the numbers are locked. But for the serious investor—the one who sees property not just as income, but as a long-term capital vehicle—this mindset is not only short-sighted, it's expensive. *The best investors don't react to taxes. They design for them.* In the right hands, taxation becomes a strategic tool—a way to compound returns, minimise friction, and preserve liquidity across time and borders.

This chapter explores that reframing in detail. We look at how depreciation, tax deferral strategies like the 1031 exchange, capital allowance structures in the UK, negative gearing in Australia, and principal residence exemptions in Canada aren't loopholes for the lucky few—they are *embedded, deliberate incentives* placed by governments to reward asset accumulation and economic contribution. The tax code, in most mature economies, is not a wall; it's a map. But you must read it well.

Let's begin with the United States, whose real estate tax code is perhaps the most sophisticated—and the most misunderstood. The single most underutilised tool in a U.S. investor's toolkit is *depreciation.* On paper, buildings deteriorate in value each year (even though most increase in market price). This 'decline' can be deducted annually from taxable income—without spending a penny. For residential property, the Internal Revenue Service allows a straight-line depreciation over 27.5 years. For commercial assets, it's 39 years. With cost segregation studies, investors can accelerate portions of that depreciation into the early years of ownership, dramatically reducing taxable income during the highest-risk phase of holding. What looks like accounting is, in reality, *a form of state-sanctioned risk mitigation.*

Even more powerful is the 1031 exchange. Named after Section 1031 of the IRS Code, this allows a property owner to sell a real estate asset and reinvest the proceeds into another like-kind property—without paying capital gains tax at the time of sale. The deferral can be rolled forward indefinitely, allowing investors to effectively redeploy wealth tax-free during their lifetime. With careful estate planning, heirs may inherit the asset with a stepped-up cost basis, eliminating the original gain entirely. The implications are enormous: *tax is not merely postponed—it can be erased.* But the process requires exacting timing, adherence to rules, and clarity of intent. Sloppy execution turns benefit into liability.

In the United Kingdom, the tax landscape differs in mechanics but not in spirit. One of the most potent advantages lies in *capital allowances*—a system by which commercial property owners can claim tax relief on qualifying expenditures within a building, such as lighting, heating systems, lifts, and air conditioning. These allowances can reduce taxable profits significantly, especially when structured correctly at acquisition. Additionally, for primary residences, the UK's principal private residence relief (PPR) can exempt most or all of a home's capital gain from tax. This creates strategic opportunity for owner-occupiers transitioning into landlords. *By understanding how a property's use class evolves, you can optimise for both lifestyle and return.*

Across the Atlantic, Canada offers a different set of levers. Here, the *principal residence exemption* also plays a central role, but with nuances. Only one property per family unit can be designated per year, meaning investors with multiple homes must plan carefully. More tactically, the Canadian Income Tax Act allows for the use of the *capital cost allowance (CCA)*—Canada's version of depreciation. But unlike the U.S., claiming CCA on a rental property eliminates your ability to shelter future gains with the principal residence exemption. This is a trade-off that must be evaluated on a time horizon: *short-term tax relief may come at the cost of long-term flexibility*. Savvy investors model both outcomes before making elections.

Australia's most contentious tax lever is *negative gearing*. When your property's expenses exceed its income, the loss can be deducted from other taxable income—effectively subsidising your investment through tax relief. This has long been criticised as a driver of speculative behaviour, but when used deliberately and in conjunction with long-term capital appreciation, it becomes a calculated play. Importantly, investors in Australia must also be aware of the *Capital Gains Tax (CGT) discount,* which reduces the taxable portion of gains by 50% if the property is held for more than 12 months. What appears at first as penalty—capital gains—can, with modest holding discipline, become a strategic advantage.

These examples are not mere trivia—they reflect an underutilised mental model: *your government is your silent partner*. Whether you like it or not, the state will share in your gains, and buffer some of your losses. Smart investors don't resist this reality; they partner with it. They structure deals not just for yield and price growth, but for *tax velocity*—the rate at which money is recycled, repositioned, and retained. For instance, a property that generates strong cash flow but is fully taxable may produce less net benefit than one with moderate income but aggressive depreciation. *Surface numbers lie. After-tax numbers tell the truth.*

This lens changes how you evaluate opportunity. It pushes you to ask not, "What's the ROI?" but "What's the post-tax ROI?" It encourages structuring decisions—such as holding title in personal name versus company, or co-investing via limited partnerships. It elevates the role of tax advisers from compliance officers to strategic collaborators. And it surfaces a hard truth: *many investors are overpaying tax simply because they don't know better.*

There are ethical considerations here, too. While it is entirely legal to optimise within the bounds of the code, the line between planning and avoidance must be tread carefully. The goal is not to dodge contribution but to engage with the rules intelligently. Tax codes are not static—they evolve in response to elections, market forces, and economic priorities. What is advantageous today may become a trap tomorrow. Investors must remain adaptive, and, where possible, *design portfolios with legislative resilience.* That might mean diversifying across asset classes, holding periods, and even jurisdictions.

Speaking of jurisdictions, the globalisation of investment portfolios has added complexity—but also optionality. Investors today are increasingly cross-border: living in one country, holding assets in another, holding passports in both. Tax treaties between nations—such as the UK-U.S. or Canada-Australia agreements—govern how income is taxed and what credits apply. Double taxation can be avoided, but only if the structure is correct. Missteps can be costly. Ignorance here is not just dangerous—it's ruinous.

Equally important is the *timing of taxation.* Real estate is uniquely suited to deferred gains and controllable recognition. Unlike equity markets, where gains are triggered at the moment of sale, real estate often allows you to choose when and how gains are realised. This provides flexibility in managing personal income tax brackets, estate plans, and cash needs. For example, a strategic refinance allows equity extraction without triggering capital gains, effectively turning growth into tax-free liquidity. *It's not about avoiding tax—it's about controlling the calendar on which it's paid.*

At its core, viewing taxes as strategy rather than burden means integrating tax into every layer of decision-making—from deal selection to structuring to exit. It means asking questions early: What is the best way to hold this asset? What incentives exist for capital upgrades? Will this be a hold or a flip, and how does that change my tax exposure? Do I need liquidity or long-term sheltering? How do I use losses from one asset to offset gains in another? The answers to these questions do not lie in the property brochure—they lie in the tax code.

The ultimate insight here is both simple and powerful: *tax is not separate from return—it is part of it.* Just as location, leverage, and cash flow shape an investment's character, so too does its tax profile. A mediocre property, well-structured, can outperform a great one mishandled. Taxes are not static charges—they are variables. And for those who learn to manipulate those variables with intelligence, discipline, and a long view, the rewards can be compounding, generational, and deeply liberating.

You do not need to be a tax lawyer to wield this power. But you must respect it. You must cultivate a mindset that sees the code not as something to fear, but as something to understand. Taxes are not the enemy of wealth—they are the language through which wealth speaks to the state. Learn to speak it fluently.

The Global Landscape of Real Estate Taxation

A property may have four walls, a postcode, and a roof—but from a tax perspective, its identity is deeply shaped by where it stands. In real estate investing, geography is not just about neighbourhoods or school districts. It's also about jurisdictional advantage—how a country's tax code either encourages or penalises property ownership, how it interprets gains and losses, and whether it treats your asset as a public good or a speculative bet. *Every piece of land belongs to a nation—and every nation taxes land in ways that reveal its values.*

Investors who confine themselves to a single domestic market often underestimate the strategic possibilities (and the hidden pitfalls) of that international landscape. Even those investing purely within their own country can learn from understanding how other systems work. *Thinking globally—even while buying locally—forces clarity.* Why does your government incentivise capital upgrades but not passive ownership? Why does one country allow rollovers and another does not? Why is rental income treated as earned income in some systems but not others? The answers to these questions are not academic—they directly shape your returns.

Let's begin with the United States, where the property tax regime is famously investor-friendly. Real estate in the U.S. benefits from several layered advantages: deductible mortgage interest, cost recovery via depreciation, capital gains deferral via the 1031 exchange, and, in many states, favourable treatment of passive income. But there are caveats. Local property taxes can be volatile and vary sharply by county, often adjusted annually. States like Texas and New Jersey impose substantial levies at the municipal level, creating drag on cash flow. At the federal level, gains on investment property are taxed preferentially at 15% or 20%, depending on income brackets—much lower than earned income. But depreciation recapture rules claw back some of these benefits on sale unless properly managed. *The U.S. gives you tools, but expects precision in how they are used.*

Cross the Atlantic and the UK offers a more cautious, tiered approach. While property in the UK is not as aggressively tax-sheltered as in the U.S., it does reward long-term, intentional ownership. Buy-to-let investors face stamp duty surcharges, phased-out mortgage interest relief, and capital gains tax that is distinct from ordinary income—but commercial property and certain development projects can still yield advantageous positions. Capital allowances on business-use property offer a quiet but powerful lever. For homeowners, the Principal Private Residence Relief (PPR) still protects large portions of gains when properties are sold after being lived in. What the UK system lacks in breadth, it offers in surgical specificity. *It rewards knowledge, not volume.*

Canada, often perceived as risk-averse, has its own strategic tools, especially for those with long horizons. The Canadian tax system makes sharp distinctions between primary residences and investment properties. The former enjoy a capital gains exemption; the latter, not so. But the ability to deduct mortgage interest, property taxes, maintenance, and even capital cost allowances (Canada's depreciation equivalent) means real estate remains a strong net-yield asset when managed with care. One overlooked feature is the ability to designate a principal residence retroactively for multiple years—useful when owning more than one property. However, this must be planned proactively, as switching designations has cascading effects. *In Canada, the investor must think like a chess player—positioning assets several moves ahead.*

Australia offers perhaps the most polarising example of how tax can shape a market. *Negative gearing*—where investors can deduct property losses from other income—has fuelled decades of speculative investment, pushing housing prices up and yield requirements down. Coupled with the 50% capital gains tax discount for assets held over a year, this creates a landscape where long-term holding and tax timing are integral to strategy. But reforms are always looming. Changes to negative gearing or CGT discounts could radically alter investor behaviour. The lesson here is not just technical—it's philosophical: *if your strategy depends on a fragile law, it is not a robust strategy.*

Now, pivot to Germany. Here we encounter a market structured more for renters than landlords. Capital gains are exempt if a property is held for ten years or more—a reward for long-term investment—but rental income is taxed at progressive personal income rates. Depreciation is slower and limited. Property transfer taxes vary by region but tend to be higher than in Anglo countries. While the German market is famously stable, it is also slow to yield liquidity unless the investor is highly intentional. Germany teaches restraint. *You don't speculate—you accumulate.*

Singapore offers a sharply contrasting model: high regulation, tight supply, and deliberate taxation mechanisms aimed at curbing speculation. The Additional Buyer's Stamp Duty (ABSD), which adds a surcharge on second and third properties, is a blunt but effective tool for cooling the market. Yet, tax on rental income remains moderate, and gains from sales are typically not taxed unless deemed to be "trading." The clarity of rules—even when punitive—gives strategic investors firm footing. Here, your tax outcomes are more about policy interpretation than accountancy. *Singapore doesn't reward clever loopholes—it rewards compliance with conviction.*

In the United Arab Emirates, meanwhile, the absence of property tax altogether has made Dubai a magnet for international buyers. But this lack of ongoing tax is offset by transfer fees, service charges, and legal opacity. The investor here must trade fiscal advantage for legal and regulatory diligence. While Dubai has no capital gains tax or income tax, the real cost lies in currency exposure, political risk, and regulatory variability. It is *a sandbox of opportunity, but not a place for amateurs.*

Japan is another instructive case. While often overlooked by foreign investors due to language and legal barriers, Japan offers accelerated depreciation for older buildings, significant write-offs for earthquake retrofitting and renovation, and low property taxes relative to value. However, property values depreciate quickly on paper, even when land appreciates, creating a mental inversion for Western investors. Here, *value lies in land, not structure*, and tax policy reflects that. Rental yields are stable, and long-term holding receives more tax leniency. But the market demands cultural fluency and operational commitment.

Beyond the specifics of each country, a few structural patterns emerge. Most developed economies offer some form of tax incentive for long-term holding. Most distinguish between active development and passive rental. Nearly all allow some variation of depreciation or capital expenditure deductions. And most penalise short-term trading through surtaxes, income characterisation, or transaction fees. These are not random quirks—they reflect a global policy orientation that prefers *patient capital over fast capital.* Understanding this allows investors to align their strategy with systemic momentum, rather than working against it.

One of the most underappreciated skills for international investors is learning to think in *after-tax global terms.* A 7% gross yield in Toronto is not equivalent to a 7% yield in Manchester or Dubai once local taxes, transfer fees, depreciation schedules, and cross-border treaties are applied. Tax treaties, especially, are crucial. The OECD Model Tax Convention governs how many countries structure double taxation avoidance. But practical application varies. Without precise structuring—such as using dual-residency declarations, treaty tie-breakers, and local tax representation—investors risk being taxed twice, or worse, audited in two jurisdictions.

Additionally, as governments adapt to increased cross-border capital flows, they're tightening disclosure regimes. The OECD's Common Reporting Standard (CRS), FATCA in the U.S., and similar initiatives in other regions are eroding the anonymity that once fuelled offshore strategies. This doesn't eliminate opportunity—it clarifies the rules of engagement. *Transparency is now a cost of entry, not a penalty.* Strategic investors accept this and plan accordingly.

Ultimately, thinking globally about taxation forces clarity on what kind of investor you want to be. Do you optimise for short-term yield, or for long-term compounded value? Do you want liquidity, or legacy? Are you prepared to invest in relationships—with advisers, tax professionals, local partners—or do you seek simplicity above all? There is no correct answer. But the more nuanced your understanding of tax policy across borders, the more precisely you can align your financial strategy with your personal priorities.

Global real estate taxation is not about playing the system. It's about reading the rules—and choosing your game accordingly. Where you invest determines how you earn, how you hold, how you exit, and ultimately, how you're remembered in the ledger of both capital and law. *To master real estate as a wealth vehicle, you must understand taxation not only as arithmetic, but as architecture.* And nowhere is that more evident than in the way each nation chooses to tax its land.

The Silent Killers: Vacancy, Repairs, and Inflation

Profit in real estate rarely dies a dramatic death. It erodes—quietly, predictably, and often invisibly—until what once looked like a solid investment becomes a strain on liquidity, a drain on patience, or worse, an underperforming asset dressed in the illusion of growth. This is the insidious power of what many novice investors overlook: the silent killers. Vacancy, repairs, and inflation are not footnotes in your financial model—they are gravitational forces pulling down your actual return while your spreadsheet smiles back at you. *Modelling these factors isn't optional—it's foundational.*

Let's start with vacancy—the most deceptively simple variable in the real estate equation. The common amateur assumption is binary: either the property is vacant or it's not. But professionals understand that vacancy is not merely a status—it's a cost, a pattern, and a strategic blind spot if not deliberately accounted for. For instance, a property with a 95% annual occupancy rate may sound healthy, but that five percent vacancy equates to nearly 18 days without income. In a high-leverage situation, that gap can wipe out your margin for error. More dangerously, if the vacancy is systemic—driven by seasonal demand, poor tenant retention, or misaligned pricing strategies—it compounds. *Predictable vacancies must be priced into your cash flow forecast with the same rigour you apply to mortgage interest or taxes.*

Vacancy also hides downstream costs. A month without rent is rarely just about lost income. It often includes turnover costs—cleaning, repainting, minor repairs, advertising, agent commissions, and possibly incentive offers to secure new tenants. These aren't speculative—they're structural. And yet they're often absent from the neat rows of "projected net income." Investors who model for 100% occupancy are not optimists—they are deluding themselves. A real-world model accounts for friction, not perfection.

Repairs, meanwhile, operate as the silent inflation within your own property. The most misunderstood aspect of repairs is not their cost, but their unpredictability. Investors tend to budget for the known—the boiler that's nearing the end of its life, the roof that might need replacement in five years. But what erodes your returns are the unknowns: the cracked drainage pipe that turns into mould remediation, the ageing electrical box flagged during an insurance renewal, the tenant whose pet caused structural damage disguised as wear and tear. These events are not outliers—they are the rule in long-term property ownership. *Predictable unpredictability must be embedded into your forecast.*

There is also a psychological trap around cosmetic versus structural repairs. Repainting a wall is often seen as maintenance. Replacing a cracked foundation is perceived as a rare disaster. But both draw from the same cash reserves, and both must be anticipated. One sophisticated approach used by seasoned investors is the "capex reserve model," in which a fixed percentage of gross rent—typically 10%—is diverted monthly into a segregated account for major repairs. This isn't about over-preparing; it's about respecting the cyclical nature of buildings. Materials degrade. Systems fail. And unless these eventualities are priced into your annual return model, your apparent profits are theoretical.

Then comes inflation—the most widely discussed and yet poorly integrated factor in real estate modelling. Inflation is not merely a macroeconomic headline; it is a compounding force that distorts both your expenses and your perceived returns over time. Many investors mistakenly believe that real estate is a perfect hedge against inflation. While property values and rents often rise in inflationary periods, so do insurance premiums, repair costs, labour rates, and property taxes. Worse, inflation erodes fixed cash flows. If your lease agreement locks in rents for several years without escalation clauses, then in real terms, your revenue is declining annually—even if nominal figures stay the same. *This quiet bleed is financial entropy—and it is entirely avoidable through thoughtful lease structuring.*

Sophisticated investors address this by including inflation-adjusted metrics in their performance analysis. One useful tool is the inflation-adjusted internal rate of return (IRR), which recalculates returns in real terms, not nominal ones. It forces clarity: your investment is not delivering 7% annually—it's delivering 7% minus inflation, minus volatility, minus vacancy, minus repairs. This is not pessimism. This is accounting with integrity. It is about understanding what the money actually does—not just what the numbers suggest on paper.

There's also a deeper insight here: the silent killers are not merely accounting challenges. They are philosophical markers of maturity. They test whether the investor is playing a short-term acquisition game or practising long-term stewardship. A landlord who ignores vacancy is often someone addicted to growth metrics, not sustainability. An owner who defers repairs may appear profitable for a few quarters—but is quietly accumulating deferred liability that will demand compound repayment. And one who models in nominal dollars rather than real purchasing power is not investing—they are gambling on a stable future that has never existed.

Consider this case: two investors each purchase a four-unit property with identical cash flows. One applies 100% of net cash to new acquisitions, using leverage to scale rapidly. The other sets aside 15% for capex reserves, accounts for expected vacancy, and inflation-adjusts his return projections. Five years later, both have grown. But one has a portfolio riddled with deferred maintenance, leveraged at tighter margins, and vulnerable to interest rate shifts. The other has fewer units but stronger assets, higher tenant retention, and the liquidity to weather downturns. *Which is the real investor—and which is the speculator?*

Moreover, inflation affects decision-making in subtle ways. It shifts the viability of renovation strategies, distorts construction timelines, and reshapes what constitutes a "good deal." A development project with tight margins might have made sense in a low-cost environment. Add a 20% increase in building materials and a six-month delay in permitting, and the numbers collapse. The lesson? Real estate is not a static equation. It is a dynamic system, in which external forces regularly recalibrate your assumptions.

What is the investor to do? First, stop seeking perfect numbers and start building resilient ones. This means using conservative assumptions for rent growth and generous estimates for repair costs. It means modelling at least one full month of vacancy per year, even in strong rental markets. It means using inflation-adjusted benchmarks for long-term planning. And most critically, it means treating real estate returns as a range, not a point. *Uncertainty is not an error—it is an input.*

Second, operational excellence must be part of your return strategy. Properties don't "cash flow" on their own. They must be maintained, re-evaluated, and repositioned. High vacancy is not just a market problem—it's often a management failure. Repairs are not merely expenses—they are the price of trust, tenant retention, and asset longevity. Inflation is not an excuse for poor performance—it's a test of adaptability.

Finally, remember that all real estate eventually tells the truth. The silent killers don't show up in the first month, or even the first year. But over a decade, they reveal whether your investment was robust or merely lucky. They separate the spreadsheet optimists from the operators. They reward those who planned for failure—and punish those who assumed their spreadsheet was reality.

So model for messiness. Build in buffers. Respect entropy. And most of all, think like a steward, not just an owner. The silent killers are only dangerous when ignored. When accounted for, they become what they've always been: the real cost of real returns.

Chapter 8
Managing What You Own (So It Doesn't Own You)

Ownership in real estate doesn't conclude with acquisition—it commences there. The day you pocket the keys is not a triumphant end-point but the beginning of something more demanding: stewardship. Buying a property calls for vision and valuation; managing it requires discipline, foresight, and the patience to design systems that last. What you hold in your portfolio can either serve you faithfully or bend your life subtly around its demands. The dividing line is rarely the property itself—it is the management. The art here is not about being perpetually busy but about being intentional, structured, and shrewd.

It's easy to buy into the fantasy—the landlord on a beach, espresso in hand, rent rolling in without interruption. The story lingers because it sells well on stages and in podcasts. Yet the lived reality is messier. Property management is anything but passive. Even with reliable tenants, watertight leases, and decent contractors, real estate tugs at your attention. Not every hour, but persistently. The task isn't to remove involvement altogether but to lift it—to move from firefighting to deliberate architecture.

The foundation of good management lies first in tenants and contracts. More than bricks or location, it's often the people and the paperwork that shape the investment's character. Good tenants don't arrive by accident; they are drawn by clarity, selected through rigour, and retained through fairness. Poor contracts, meanwhile, are the breeding ground of disputes. The seasoned landlord knows a precise clause can prevent more friction than any future argument. Take something as simple as access rights: spell out inspection frequency and conditions, and you avert tension later. Contracts drafted with care aren't merely legal shields; they are pre-emptive conversations.

But paperwork won't carry the weight alone. Effective management requires a mindset shift—particularly around maintenance. Too often seen as a dull expense, maintenance is better regarded as the craft of asset preservation and a quiet gesture of respect toward tenants. Preventive care is rarely dramatic, but it's powerful: leaks contained before they spread, boilers serviced before they collapse. Neglect compounds invisibly, while attentiveness accrues dividends. A wise investor treats maintenance not as cost avoidance but as strategic investment.

Of course, trying to shoulder it all personally is a recipe for exhaustion. Many first-time investors fall into the trap of equating self-reliance with control. Yet delegation, done well, is not abdication. Bringing in property managers, contractors, or assistants should widen your bandwidth, not dilute your authority. The secret lies in structure: clear scopes, defined expectations, measurable outcomes. A competent manager can free your focus for higher-level decisions. A poor one, by contrast, can transform an asset into a liability. The art is in choosing selectively, trusting carefully, and measuring consistently.

And still—mistakes will happen. A tenant disappoints. A contractor cuts corners. You miss a recurring charge in the annual budget or approve a repair that could have been avoided. These aren't signs that you've failed; they're simply the tuition fees of experience. What matters is not avoiding error altogether, but tightening the loop between error and correction. Missteps become ruinous only when ignored or repeated. Those who mature in the role of ownership log their lessons, adapt their systems, and seek patterns rather than scapegoats. In property, humility outperforms perfectionism.

It's worth noting too how management reshapes the manager. Handling property doesn't just alter your balance sheet—it alters you. Negotiation sharpens. Logistics become second nature. Emotional discipline hardens. A midnight call from a tenant with a burst pipe is more than a practical nuisance; it's a test of composure and principle. A decision about a cosmetic upgrade is not just financial—it's an exercise in reading markets, sensing style, and positioning strategically. Property management, if taken seriously, is a crucible in which the investor matures.

Left unchecked, however, management can consume its master. A portfolio that expands faster than its systems mutates into a parasite. The warnings are subtle: inboxes filling with maintenance requests, weekends vanishing to tenant coordination, receipts piling up unsorted. Growth amplifies whatever already exists—competence or chaos. Those who endure don't just acquire more properties; they build systems first. They know each acquisition adds responsibility alongside revenue. Scale without structure erodes sanity.

This chapter, then, offers something practical. It teaches how to draw in and keep quality tenants, using methods refined by those who have survived the pitfalls. It shows how to draft leases that preserve clarity without poisoning goodwill. It reframes maintenance from cost to philosophy. It equips you to navigate the tricky ecosystem of managers and contractors while retaining command. And it shares stories of error and repair—reminders that mastery is iterative, not instantaneous.

Managing what you own isn't about chasing perfection or clinging to a myth of "hands-off" wealth. It is about crafting systems that resonate with your values, your life, and your financial design. It is about leaning into the role of owner—not in name only, but in practice and principle. Done with intention, property management ceases to be a burden and becomes leverage. It grants you control while you grow, clarity as you operate, and integrity as you own. That is the promise: not theory but lived mastery—earned, adjusted, and folded into every decision beyond the day you first turned the key.

Tenants, Contracts, and Clear Boundaries:

Few aspects of property investment generate as much long-term consequence—and as much emotional volatility—as tenants. For many first-time landlords, the learning curve is steep: the ideal tenant is not simply one who pays rent on time, but one who upholds the property's condition, communicates proactively, respects boundaries, and aligns with the long-term value of the asset. Yet attracting such tenants doesn't happen by chance. It is engineered through intentional design—starting with the screening process and codified in contracts that do far more than list obligations. *Clarity is the antidote to conflict—and in the world of property management, ambiguity is expensive.*

Before any discussion of lease clauses or screening checklists, it is vital to understand the foundational psychology at play. A lease is not merely a legal agreement; it is a boundary-setting device between two parties with potentially diverging interests. Many novice landlords assume goodwill is enough. It isn't. Verbal agreements dissolve under stress, and even well-meaning tenants can misinterpret expectations when they are not explicitly stated. The landlord-tenant relationship is a professional one and should be governed by documented clarity, not informal assumptions.

Quality tenants are rarely discovered through luck. They are attracted through a process that signals professionalism from the very first contact. This begins with a listing that is honest, specific, and structured. Listings that over-promise, under-define, or omit critical information often serve as magnets for the very behaviour landlords hope to avoid. An advertisement that clearly outlines rent, deposit, lease term, permitted uses, and even tenant qualifications—such as income requirements or credit expectations—saves both parties from unnecessary friction. *Specificity isn't rigidity; it's a signal of seriousness.*

Once inquiries come in, the screening process must balance legal compliance with discernment. While local housing laws will dictate what you can and cannot ask—particularly regarding discrimination protections—there is still ample room for intelligent filtering. Bank statements, proof of income, references from previous landlords, and credit reports are standard. But experienced landlords go further: they assess consistency in answers, communication timeliness, and tone. Patterns reveal character. A tenant who reschedules repeatedly or is vague about their employment history may introduce administrative entropy that compounds over time.

Even with a strong candidate, the lease agreement itself becomes the ultimate risk mitigation tool. Too often, first-time investors use template leases pulled from the internet, unaware that much of the protective nuance is buried in what they exclude. For instance, one frequently overlooked clause relates to routine inspections. A professionally crafted lease will clearly state the landlord's right to inspect the premises periodically—typically with a minimum notice period—and the purpose of those visits (e.g., maintenance, safety checks). *This clause alone can deter neglect and serve as early detection against property misuse.*

Another critical clause involves maintenance responsibility. Vague language such as "tenant to keep premises clean and in good order" is legally frail and practically unenforceable. A stronger clause would read: *'Tenant shall be responsible for maintaining cleanliness and order in all interior areas, including kitchen, bathrooms, and shared spaces, and shall immediately report any structural, electrical, or plumbing faults to the landlord in writing within 48 hours of discovery.* "This level of specificity places the onus where it belongs, while protecting the landlord against 'deferred maintenance defence'—where tenants claim ignorance of developing issues.

Late payment penalties, subletting restrictions, pet policies, smoking bans, and noise expectations should all be stated in detail. But equally important is the tone of the lease. Legalese can create distance; clear, human-readable English inspires understanding and compliance. Where possible, it helps to include a preamble—a brief paragraph explaining that the lease is designed to create fairness, protect the property, and preserve a professional relationship. Many tenants, especially those unfamiliar with formal agreements, interpret long contracts as antagonistic. Framing the document as mutual protection can help align both parties from the outset.

Beyond documentation, effective boundaries are reinforced through management practices. Tenants respond not just to rules, but to consistency. If you state in the lease that noise complaints will be followed up within 48 hours, then fail to act for a week, you erode your own authority. The same applies to late fees, repair scheduling, and renewal procedures. Professional landlords adopt the mindset of systems rather than reaction. *Predictability builds trust. Inconsistency breeds resentment.*

Case studies illustrate how lack of boundaries can spiral into disproportionate costs. Consider the landlord who verbally agreed to let a tenant "keep a friend over occasionally," only to discover that the property was being informally sublet on Airbnb. With no clause prohibiting subletting and no paper trail of the verbal agreement, legal recourse was difficult and drawn-out. Or take the case of a landlord who trusted a tenant's promise to "handle minor repairs," only to find years later that improper plumbing work caused substantial water damage—damage not covered by insurance due to unauthorised modifications. These aren't rare exceptions; they are recurring scenarios in the absence of contractual clarity.

That said, contracts are not blunt instruments. The most successful property owners understand that enforcing every rule without discretion can be counterproductive. A late rent payment during a tenant's medical emergency may warrant compassion. A consistently respectful long-term tenant who adopts a rescue pet might be worth accommodating—even if it means modifying your pet policy. But the crucial point is this: flexibility is most powerful when it is a *choice*, not a default. Clear contracts allow you to extend grace when appropriate—without sacrificing the structure that makes such discretion sustainable.

Some landlords hesitate to assert firm boundaries for fear of deterring good tenants. This is a miscalculation. Good tenants value clarity because it protects them, too. A tenant who has lived through a negligent landlord or shared space with unpredictable co-tenants will appreciate a well-defined structure that safeguards their peace and predictability. *Boundaries are not barriers to goodwill; they are the framework in which goodwill can flourish.*

Technology has further enabled smart contract management. Digital lease platforms, automated reminders, and online maintenance request portals reduce friction and improve documentation. But technology cannot replace judgment. Knowing when to re-negotiate a lease term, when to evict, or when to increase rent in alignment with market trends still requires human reasoning. The art of property management lies in balancing precision with empathy—and knowing which lever to pull in which moment.

Ultimately, a well-managed property begins with a well-managed relationship—and relationships, even contractual ones, are defined by expectations and respect. Contracts are not mere paperwork. They are signals. They shape the tone, tenor, and trajectory of how a property performs as an investment. When crafted thoughtfully and enforced consistently, they become not a line of defence, but a platform for peace of mind. *And in real estate, peace of mind is a form of profit.*

Repairs and the Psychology of Maintenance:

A leaking tap rarely announces itself as a philosophical lesson. A cracked tile or rattling boiler seldom evokes introspection. But the experienced investor recognises these signs not just as functional faults, but as signals—early expressions of entropy that, left unacknowledged, begin to unravel both property and profit. Preventive maintenance is often framed as a matter of practicality or cost efficiency. Yet beneath the surface lies a deeper truth: *how you care for your asset reflects how seriously you regard it.* Maintenance is not simply upkeep—it is stewardship. And stewardship, unlike passive ownership, demands attention, humility, and pattern recognition.

Many first-time property investors approach maintenance reactively. They respond only when tenants complain, or when something fails so visibly that inaction becomes impossible. This mindset is not just inefficient—it is financially reckless. Deferred maintenance leads to compounding problems. A small roof leak allowed to persist through two rainy seasons becomes structural rot. A faulty water heater, left unchecked, results in mould remediation and tenant dissatisfaction. *Minor neglect accumulates into major cost.* The investor who waits for repairs to become urgent is not saving money—they are borrowing against the future.

But even beyond cost, there is a more subtle danger in reactive maintenance: the slow erosion of psychological clarity. A property that is visibly deteriorating—even in marginal, cosmetic ways—changes the posture of its inhabitants. A scuffed wall, an unrepaired gate, or a loose handrail signals, however unconsciously, a lack of order. Tenants perceive this. So do neighbours. And so, crucially, does the landlord. The property begins to feel burdensome. Each small imperfection chips away at the original confidence of ownership. It becomes harder to take pride in the asset, and with diminished pride comes diminished discipline. *What isn't respected isn't protected.*

Preventive maintenance, by contrast, is an act of intentionality. It is about creating a calendar—not just reacting to a crisis. Savvy investors implement quarterly checklists: gutters cleaned before autumn, HVAC systems serviced annually, windows resealed before winter, smoke alarms tested regularly. They treat the property not as a static structure, but as a living system with cycles and needs. More than this, they involve tenants in the process—establishing clear reporting protocols, educating them on what to observe, and setting expectations for access during inspections. *A tenant who sees the landlord taking care of the property feels more compelled to do the same.*

Yet, it is important to acknowledge that not all maintenance is equal. There is a crucial distinction between cosmetic perfectionism and structural stewardship. A minor scratch on a benchtop may be worth accepting; a damp patch in the ceiling never is. Understanding the hierarchy of urgency allows owners to triage repairs with discipline, not paranoia. This requires technical literacy—not becoming a tradesperson, but learning enough to ask intelligent questions and spot misdirection from unscrupulous contractors. The investor who cannot distinguish between rising damp and a condensation issue will either overspend or under-react. Both paths are costly.

Equally, there is a philosophical shift that occurs when maintenance is reframed from obligation to ritual. In many cultures, regular upkeep of a home is not just practical but moral. Japanese property culture, for example, emphasises continuous renewal through cleanliness and minor daily interventions. While Western markets often fixate on value appreciation through upgrades or flips, some of the world's most resilient property owners adopt a mindset of *preservation through attentiveness*. This isn't mysticism—it's risk management wrapped in care.

It also aligns with a deeper financial principle. Maintenance sustains—not just the physical condition of the asset, but its ability to command higher rents, lower tenant turnover, and positive reputational spillover. A property that looks well-kept doesn't merely retain value—it *attracts* value. It appeals to conscientious tenants, passes inspections with fewer issues, and—should the time come—commands a premium in sale negotiations. These are not secondary benefits; they are strategic outcomes. *Preventive care is not cost—it is margin disguised as expense.*

Critically, owners must be cautious about the psychology of avoidance. Many resist addressing minor issues out of fear of discovering major ones. The assumption is that what they don't know can't hurt them. But it can. Investors must confront their discomfort. Regular inspections, thorough documentation, and transparent repair histories are not optional—they are tools of agency. And agency is the opposite of anxiety.

Consider the real-world example of two identical flats purchased in the same block. One landlord conducts annual servicing of the boiler, repaints every three years, and keeps a modest sinking fund for upgrades. The other adopts a "wait and see" model. After seven years, the difference in value, tenant satisfaction, and maintenance burden is dramatic. One flat attracts long-term professional tenants and retains 98% occupancy. The other suffers frequent complaints, rent stagnation, and eventually requires £15,000 in emergency upgrades that could have been avoided for a fraction of the cost. Same postcode. Same floor plan. Entirely different philosophies.

Maintenance also intersects with ethics. A landlord who neglects repairs not only jeopardises their bottom line—they fail in their duty of care. Safe, functional housing is not just a market product; it is a social contract. Investors must hold themselves to standards beyond mere compliance. This is not a moralistic plea; it is a long-term investment thesis. Responsible ownership builds goodwill with tenants, regulators, and communities. That goodwill, in turn, becomes resilience—against legal threats, reputational damage, and vacancies. *Reputation is a capital asset, and it is maintained just like plumbing: through routine attention.*

Finally, the question of delegation arises. Should maintenance be handled personally or outsourced? There is no universal answer, but there is a universal rule: *delegation is not abdication.* Whether using a property manager or a set of trusted tradespeople, the owner must remain strategically involved. Review invoices. Ask for before-and-after photos. Understand what was fixed and why. Owners who blindly hand off maintenance to third parties often discover, too late, that corners were cut—or worse, that costs were inflated without justification. Vigilance need not mean micromanagement. But it does mean presence.

The most successful property investors do not view repairs as interruptions to their investment plan. They see them as *integral to it.* Each act of maintenance is an opportunity to reaffirm control, preserve value, and communicate expectations. Maintenance, at its best, is a philosophy—one rooted in respect for the asset, the occupants, and the future. It is the daily discipline that underpins long-term advantage. And those who embrace it will find that their properties not only last—they lead.

"Hiring Help Without Losing Control":

No investor scales without delegation. But no investor survives without discernment. The line between wise outsourcing and dangerous abdication is perilously thin, and many well-meaning property owners have crossed it—lured by convenience, trapped by dependency. Whether it's a property manager promising effortless income, a contractor quoting urgent repairs, or an estate agent guiding a sale, the lesson is universal: *hire help, but never surrender control.* Control is not about micromanagement—it's about informed oversight, structural clarity, and strategic agency.

The temptation to offload responsibility intensifies as portfolios grow. Early-stage landlords, juggling full-time careers or family demands, understandably seek relief from the operational grind. And with the right hires, that relief can evolve into a robust system. But systems are only as strong as their feedback loops. Blind trust—especially in the property sector—is not a virtue. It's a liability. *The cost of ignorance is rarely immediate—but always cumulative.*

Start with property managers. The promise of "hands-free" management is seductive: they'll handle rent collection, repairs, tenant screening, compliance, and even disputes. But investors who interpret "hands-free" as "eyes-off" soon lose touch with their asset's performance. Many don't know if rents are market-aligned, if tenants are happy, or if maintenance costs are creeping upward. When issues emerge, they're often downstream of years of passive disengagement. The antidote is not to avoid hiring—but to hire with clarity.

A skilled investor sets expectations from the outset, building a framework for accountability. Contracts should detail service scope, response times, cost thresholds for repairs, and communication protocols. And these are not templates to be passively accepted. They are strategic documents to be negotiated and revised. *Control begins with contract design.* For example, avoid vague clauses like "reasonable maintenance costs." Instead, specify that repairs exceeding a fixed sum (say £300) require written approval. Define what constitutes an emergency. Clarify how often financial reports will be delivered and in what format.

Then there's the human side of oversight. Investors must cultivate the habit of proactive engagement. Quarterly performance reviews with managers. Random property visits. Periodic conversations with tenants (directly or via anonymous surveys) to sense-check whether promises align with experience. *Professional doesn't mean invisible. And distance is not the same as detachment.* Landlords who stay curious—without being controlling—tend to spot inefficiencies before they metastasise.

Contractors require a different approach. Their work is task-specific, often time-sensitive, and rich in information asymmetry. Most landlords cannot verify the necessity or quality of a proposed fix—at least not without effort. This vulnerability is a breeding ground for mispricing, shortcuts, and scope creep. The only antidote is structured transparency. Require itemised quotes. Ask for photographic evidence before and after. Cross-check pricing against online trade databases or competitor quotes. Over time, you'll build a trusted network—but until then, vigilance is the cost of protection.

And beware the "urgent fix" narrative. If a contractor consistently discovers major faults that require immediate resolution, treat it as a pattern worth investigating—not as an excuse to rush approval. *Speed should follow validation—not replace it.*

With estate agents, the risks centre more around alignment than expertise. Their interests are often transaction-driven: close the deal, claim the fee, move on. But for investors, long-term asset selection is far more consequential than fast turnover. The wrong neighbourhood, poor yield, or low-quality tenants can sabotage a portfolio for years. Thus, investors must cultivate *advisors*, not just agents. Choose professionals who demonstrate market literacy, not just sales patter. Probe their analysis: why this street? What are the local rent trends? What demographic are we targeting? How did you verify those comparables?

And don't be afraid to interrogate the data. Many agents offer only surface-level metrics—price per square foot, past sale prices, or glossy brochures. The sophisticated investor asks for deeper layers: time-on-market analysis, vendor discount trends, nearby planning applications, school catchment effects. *Your questions signal your standards. And your standards shape the service you receive.*

Across all these roles, a common principle emerges: hire specialists, but retain strategic authority. This doesn't mean doing everything yourself. It means remaining intellectually involved. The investor who understands basic building systems, lettings law, and financial modelling isn't trying to become a plumber, solicitor, or accountant—they're *fortifying their judgement.* And fortified judgement is what prevents exploitation.

There's also a psychological layer. Many new investors fear confrontation. They avoid questioning fees, challenging poor communication, or replacing underperforming hires. They equate assertiveness with conflict. But what's at stake is not etiquette—it's capital. You are the client. You are the steward of the asset. And stewardship requires *courageous clarity.* Every missed follow-up, every unchallenged invoice, every silently tolerated delay is a micro-deposit in the account of disempowerment.

Of course, there is a spectrum. Micromanagement is just as corrosive as disengagement. Constant interference demoralises skilled professionals and creates bottlenecks. The goal is not surveillance—it's partnership with accountability. Structure creates freedom. When roles, rules, and reporting are well-defined, trust can grow naturally. But *unearned trust is a tax you don't see until the audit arrives.*

Real-world examples illuminate this. Consider the landlord who allowed a property manager to self-approve all maintenance up to £1,000, with no cap on frequency. Over three years, the property logged more than £25,000 in repairs—many of them cosmetic, duplicated, or poorly timed. The landlord never checked the invoices until refinancing triggered a portfolio audit. The result: delayed goals, lender scrutiny, and tenant turnover due to disruptive works. Contrast that with an owner who capped pre-approval at £250, required monthly summaries, and reviewed tenant feedback semi-annually. Their maintenance costs were 40% lower, with significantly higher retention. *Same market. Different management. Divergent results.*

The long-term investor approaches delegation like a CEO assembling a leadership team. Each hire extends their reach, not dilutes their oversight. And like any good CEO, the investor builds dashboards: rent collection ratios, vacancy days, maintenance spend as a percentage of income, tenant satisfaction scores. These metrics, when tracked over time, reveal not just performance—but patterns. *And pattern recognition is the highest form of leverage.*

To hire help without losing control is not just a tactical skill—it is a mindset. It requires the humility to admit you can't do everything yourself, and the discipline to stay connected anyway. It demands clear contracts, ongoing communication, and the willingness to replace underperformers when necessary. It invites systems thinking—not just people pleasing. Because while great help multiplies your time, misplaced trust compounds your risk. *Your name is on the deed. Your capital is on the line. And your decisions shape the future of your portfolio.*

Living With—and Learning From—Your Mistakes

Mistakes in property investment are not symptoms of failure—they are signals. They whisper truths that spreadsheets obscure, lessons that inspection reports don't warn about, and insights that surface only after your assumptions have been tested by the friction of reality. For the thoughtful investor, errors are not blemishes to be hidden but opportunities for calibration. The mistake is not that a boiler failed; it's that you never factored the lifespan of the system into your yield model. The error isn't the dodgy tenant—it's that you ignored your own screening criteria because the rent looked good on paper. *Real wisdom in property doesn't come from avoiding mistakes—it comes from metabolising them into better judgment.*

Many new investors approach their first deal with a cocktail of optimism and spreadsheet precision. Forecasts look elegant, assumptions feel rational, and margins seem sufficient. But investing is not a lab experiment. The real world introduces variables you hadn't modelled: a local council that delays permits, a tradesperson who vanishes mid-project, or a tenant who knows how to game every loophole in the lease. These aren't just annoyances; they're thresholds. How you respond—whether defensively, reactively, or reflectively—shapes your evolution from amateur to competent operator.

Consider a case study: a mid-career professional, new to investing, acquires a semi-detached property in a "transitional" neighbourhood. The numbers work: strong rental demand, minor cosmetic upgrades, decent yield on paper. But within months, it becomes clear the block is fraught with noise complaints, social tensions, and nightly police visits. Instead of admitting misjudgment, the investor doubles down—blaming tenants, overrenovating, trying to polish a fundamentally mismatched asset. Eventually, the investor sells at a loss. The mistake wasn't the neighbourhood per se; it was the failure to match the property's dynamics with personal capacity. *Lesson learned: the best investors don't only analyse properties—they analyse themselves.*

Property management demands emotional discipline. The need for control often disguises itself as competence, but rigidity is not the same as strength. A landlord who refuses to hire a manager out of fear of losing oversight often ends up spending 20 hours a week doing work worth £12 an hour—eroding strategic focus and, ultimately, performance. Conversely, blind outsourcing without understanding the mechanics can make you a hostage to others' incompetence or incentives. One investor delegated everything to a property manager without vetting their contractor network. Repairs became a profit centre. £60 door handles. £700 tap fixes. When the landlord reviewed the invoices months later, the financial damage had already calcified into the portfolio's operating costs. *The corrective insight here is not "never outsource" but "never outsource blind."*

Every mistake carries both a financial cost and a cognitive dividend. The trick is not to minimise the former at the expense of the latter. One of the most instructive errors is overcapitalisation—spending £40,000 on a kitchen renovation in a £250,000 rental in a working-class suburb where laminate benches and durable finishes would have sufficed. Investors rationalise the spend: better tenants, higher rent, fewer repairs. But the local market won't always reward aesthetic ambition. The long-term payback is stretched, and the resale value may still be benchmarked against nearby, less-polished comparables. *Here, humility—not aesthetic pride—should have been the design brief.*

Sometimes the most dangerous mistakes are not made in haste but in fatigue. After dozens of viewings and near-misses, many investors talk themselves into lowering their bar. "This one is good enough." "Maybe that roof issue isn't such a big deal." "The tenant's situation is only temporary." But desperation clouds judgment like fog over a harbour—it makes familiar landmarks disappear. A seasoned investor will often walk away from a superficially appealing deal simply because it doesn't fit the playbook, no matter how tired or impatient they feel. *Discipline is not just about saying no to bad deals—it's about saying no to deals that are merely not terrible.*

The value of pattern recognition cannot be overstated. Experienced investors don't merely react to red flags—they anticipate them. They've seen how a lack of off-street parking affects long-term tenant retention. They understand how the proximity to a nightclub affects resale demand. They've learned, often painfully, that buying a property with an enthusiastic seller and no solicitor yet retained is a recipe for post-agreement delays and buyer's remorse. These are not anecdotes—they are data points acquired the hard way. *Wisdom in real estate is accumulative—but only if you're paying attention.*

One lesser-discussed but powerful mistake is neglecting personal bandwidth. Some investors build portfolios that scale in numbers but collapse in complexity. Four well-positioned, low-maintenance properties can outperform eight high-yield but management-intensive units. But spreadsheets rarely capture cognitive drag: the stress of four weekly tenant calls, managing multiple repairs, or resolving disputes across jurisdictions. An ambitious investor may hit a wall not because of bad properties, but because the business model was too brittle for their life structure. *Sustainable investing is not just about portfolio yield—it's about personal durability.*

A compelling example of redemption comes from an investor who overleveraged during a rising market. Flush with confidence after two successful flips, he took on three concurrent renovations with short-term finance. When the market cooled, he was caught mid-project, with evaporating margins and mounting bridge loan interest. Instead of folding or selling under pressure, he negotiated extended terms, partnered with a builder on deferred payment, and converted one project into a long-term hold. Five years later, the properties became his foundation for financial freedom—not because he timed the market perfectly, but because he managed the aftermath honourably. *It's not the error that defines you—it's the architecture of your recovery.*

There's a particular kind of courage required to admit, document, and dissect your own missteps. Investors who keep detailed post-mortems—spreadsheets tracking variance from expected rents, maintenance costs, or project timelines—build intellectual compounding into their model. This isn't naval-gazing; it's enterprise-level thinking. Large real estate firms have entire departments dedicated to project debriefs. Individual investors can emulate this with a Google Doc and an hour of honest reflection per quarter. *You don't need to be a genius to succeed—you need to be willing to learn out loud.*

The investor who pretends they never err isn't inspiring—they're dangerous. Mistakes are not a detour from the process; they are the process. A mature investor culture must celebrate not just returns, but reflection. Owning your misjudgements gives you authority. Sharing them gives you credibility. Learning from them gives you leverage. This is the quiet competency that separates a portfolio built on luck from one built to last.

Let the bruises become your textbooks. Let regret fuel refinement. And above all, keep the receipts—not just for taxes, but for truth.

Chapter 9
Protecting and Passing On What You Build:

There is a quiet paradox at the core of property investment: the longer you practise it successfully, the less it centres on you. What might begin as a quest for cash flow, appreciation, or portfolio size eventually pushes you into a reckoning with permanence. Bricks weather. Markets tilt. Yet the frameworks you put in place—legal, financial, even cultural—may last far beyond the numbers that first drew you in.

Wealth left unstructured is brittle; structure built without purpose is lifeless. This chapter starts where many investors eventually, and often inadvertently, arrive: with something not only to own, but to safeguard and to pass forward. Whether you hold a modest buy-to-let flat or a sprawl of properties across borders, you have taken on stewardship of more than assets. You are shaping continuity. Asset protection—through legal scaffolding, careful insurance, succession planning—is not mere paperwork. It is design work of the highest order. Yet too many dismiss it, assuming a will is enough, or trusting heirs—or the state—to settle the matter. That neglect can unravel everything: lawsuits, probate entanglements, fractured families, punitive tax bills. These are not abstractions. They are the inevitable outcomes of leaving legacy to chance.

We begin, then, with the architecture of protection. Limited liability companies, land trusts, layered insurance, cross-border tax shields—these are not magic tricks but instruments, each with a logic, a place, and a cost. We will weigh how different legal climates—from America's litigation-heavy ethos to Britain's traditions of trust and inheritance—shape what you can and should deploy. The point here is not a catalogue of loopholes, but a framework for identifying your vulnerabilities and crafting resilience from the ground up.

Yet frameworks alone will not preserve meaning. Protection is as much about the narrative of wealth as about its legal custody. In the section on intergenerational thinking, we will examine the stories that cling to property: about ownership, duty, entitlement. Why do some dynasties hold estates for centuries, while others watch them dissolve in a single generation? The answer is rarely just financial engineering. Culture does more work than accountants admit. In Japan, passing homes through generations is nearly a given; in southern Europe, family estates anchor identity. In North America, inheritance tax and a culture of individualism often sever the thread early. These contrasts matter, whether you expect to have heirs or not, because they reveal both constraints and creative openings.

And property is never only financial. It is lived space, imbued with memory and sentiment. That emotional charge can paralyse decisions—delaying sales, complicating gifts—or, if harnessed, it can bring clarity. What is it you hope to leave? A title deed? A windfall? Or something less tangible but more enduring: a set of values, a sense of belonging, an ethic of care? Consider the investor who signed over a building to a community trust rather than kin; the couple who laced donation clauses into their titles; the landlord who sold everything and left a letter instead. None chose the same path, and none was wrong. The virtue lay in asking the right question.

In the end, legacy stretches beyond land. When you have built well—bought wisely, protected intelligently, managed with competence—the properties themselves fade in importance. They become a medium. For some, that medium secures a bloodline; for others, it enables philanthropy, mentorship, advocacy. Legacy is not permanence—it is intention carried forward. Without it, even the most elaborate estate plan drifts like a vessel without a rudder.

This is not a chapter about sentiment. It is about seriousness. Earlier chapters guided you through acquisition and operation; this final one asks what it all amounts to. Not in theory, but in structure. Not in sentiment, but in purpose. Whether your ambition is to soften inheritance tax, gift strategically, or carve out an enduring platform through trusts or endowments, the thinking begins here—with sharp questions, practical mechanisms, and respect for what you have already built.

By its close, you will be prepared to do more than conserve wealth. You will be ready to define it, to name it, to guide it. And to ensure that what you have laboured to create does not merely persist, but persists with integrity.

Wealth Without Worry: Legal Structures and Protections:

It is not wealth alone that secures peace of mind—it is structure. Property investors often spend years mastering acquisition strategies, optimising yields, and scaling portfolios, only to discover that what truly protects their wealth is what happens *after* the purchase. Ownership, absent deliberate architecture, invites vulnerability. Lawsuits, tax erosion, mismanagement, and family conflict do not stem from bad fortune. More often, they stem from *vague ownership, absent planning, or misplaced trust.* The most financially successful investors are not just good buyers—they are exceptional designers of legal frameworks. This subchapter explores those frameworks: the logic behind limited liability, the silent work of insurance, and the deeply human dimensions of inheritance law. Not as abstract legal theory, but as precise, applicable, and indispensable components of any serious property strategy.

To begin, let us be clear: the purpose of legal structuring is not to dodge responsibility—it is to *contain risk*. Holding property in your personal name might be convenient, but it is structurally naive. If a tenant slips on a stair, if a contractor sues for breach, or if a fire exposes gaps in coverage, you are personally liable. Your wages, your home, even your savings—on the table. The fix is not panic; it is *incorporation.* In the United States, this takes the form of Limited Liability Companies (LLCs). In the United Kingdom, Special Purpose Vehicles (SPVs) or limited companies serve a similar role. Canada offers corporations and trusts; Australia favours discretionary trusts and self-managed superannuation funds (SMSFs). The label changes by jurisdiction, but the principle holds: *separating the asset from the individual protects both.* This is not mere legalism—it is foundational strategy.

Still, forming an entity is not a panacea. Too often, novice investors form an LLC or company without understanding the governance it requires. Annual filings, tax treatment, capital structure—these are not passive details. For instance, placing multiple properties into a single LLC may defeat the purpose of risk segregation. A fire in one building can jeopardise the entire portfolio. Similarly, failing to distinguish between personal and business accounts can trigger "piercing the corporate veil"—a legal mechanism by which courts disregard your protections. *Asset protection only works when the entity is treated as real—not just on paper, but in behaviour, records, and intention.*

Insurance, meanwhile, is frequently misunderstood as a transactional product. In practice, it is a *customisable shield.* Beyond basic property coverage, serious investors should consider landlord liability, business interruption, loss of rent, and umbrella policies. In litigious jurisdictions like the U.S., umbrella liability coverage is especially prudent—extending protection beyond standard limits, often at surprisingly low cost. But coverage without review is as risky as no coverage at all. Policy exclusions—mould, flood, vacancy clauses—often hide in the footnotes. The most experienced property owners review their policies annually, not just to adjust premiums, but to recalibrate against the actual evolution of their risk. An apartment above a commercial bakery, for instance, introduces fire and liability exposures that a standard residential policy may not address. *Risk, like property, evolves. So must your coverage.*

Tax strategy, too, is a form of legal protection—*not just from the taxman, but from value erosion over time.* Countries vary widely in their treatment of real estate income and gains. In the U.S., depreciation allows investors to deduct a portion of the property's value annually, reducing taxable income without reducing actual cash flow. This phantom expense can be powerful—but only if tracked, reported, and recaptured correctly. In the U.K., mortgage interest relief has been gradually curtailed, changing the calculus for landlords who hold properties in their own names. Canada taxes capital gains on 50% of realised profits, while Australia offers generous CGT discounts for long-term holdings and favourable treatment through SMSFs. The message is not to memorise these mechanics—it is to *internalise that tax strategy is jurisdiction-specific, structure-dependent, and time-sensitive.* Ignoring it is not conservative; it is careless.

But legal structure is not only about avoiding external threats—it is also a bulwark against *internal disorder.* Family partnerships, unclear wills, or ambiguous succession plans have destroyed more wealth than recessions or regulation. Inheritance law is rarely intuitive. In many jurisdictions, intestacy (dying without a valid will) leads to forced distributions that ignore your wishes. A divorced spouse may inherit against your intent; a minor child may force the sale of a property to release their share. Even among sophisticated investors, this remains one of the most neglected aspects of wealth design. The fix is not morbid—it is mature. Wills, living trusts, powers of attorney, and letters of intent are not paperwork—they are *instruments of clarity*. The best estate plans are not just tax-efficient—they are *legible, intentional, and adaptable*.

Consider a case study. In California, a landlord with three residential buildings dies unexpectedly. He had excellent insurance, an LLC, and clean financials. But he had no will. Under state law, his estranged spouse inherits two-thirds of the estate. His adult children contest the distribution. Meanwhile, the properties sit unmanaged for 18 months in probate, tenants leave, and value drops by nearly 30%. A lifetime of strategy, undone not by error, but omission. Now compare that with an investor in London who held properties in a family trust, with named beneficiaries, a corporate trustee, and a letter of wishes. Upon her death, the portfolio continues operating uninterrupted. Her values are preserved, not just her assets. *Protection, done properly, is continuity in motion.*

Yet there is nuance. Over-structuring can backfire. Holding each property in a separate entity may maximise protection, but it can also complicate financing, tax filings, and operational coordination. Some investors build labyrinthine corporate hierarchies to shield assets—only to find themselves tangled in their own complexity. Others rely too heavily on advisors without understanding the logic themselves. This chapter does not advocate maximalism. It advocates *coherence*. The best structures balance legal robustness with operational elegance. They protect without paralysing. They adapt across generations.

Indeed, the most overlooked component of asset protection is *education*. Not yours alone—but that of your heirs, your partners, your executors. Structures fail when those who inherit them do not understand them. A trust is only as effective as the trustee is competent. An LLC is only as safe as the managers are diligent. Preparing successors to navigate these tools is not a matter of fairness—it is a matter of functionality. If your adult child will one day inherit a real estate holding company, they must understand governance, compliance, and strategic intent. If they do not, the risk is not just that they mismanage—it is that they *abdicate*, outsourcing decisions to third parties who may not share your values. *Legacy is not just what you leave behind—it is what you teach before you go.*

Ultimately, legal structuring is not about fear. It is about *freedom*. The freedom to operate without undue exposure. The freedom to focus on growth, knowing your foundations are stable. The freedom to rest, knowing that your life's work will not be undone by paperwork, litigation, or confusion. Whether you are just acquiring your first property or curating a multi-generational trust, the principles remain the same: *design before disaster; structure before scale; clarity before complexity.*

A property without legal protection is not an asset—it is a liability in disguise. A portfolio without succession is not a legacy—it is a liquidation waiting to happen. This subchapter is your blueprint for avoiding both.

Intergenerational Thinking:

One of the most striking features of property investment—often overlooked by even the most strategic minds—is that buildings tend to outlast their builders. Brick resists time in a way that equity portfolios do not. A property acquired in your forties may still be standing—and generating income—long after your obituary has been written. This simple truth should alter how one thinks about ownership. If real estate is inherently intergenerational, then property strategy must extend beyond personal timelines. Whether or not you have children, whether or not you ever intend to "pass on" anything, you are participating in a cycle that began before you and will almost certainly continue after you. *To ignore that cycle is to misunderstand the asset class.*

Around the world, different cultures internalise this principle with striking variety—and each model has something to teach the thoughtful investor. In Japan, ancestral land often remains within the same family for generations, tied not just to economic function but to familial honour and identity. In parts of India, property is distributed via extended joint families, where multiple generations cohabit or co-manage, reflecting collectivist priorities. In contrast, Anglo-American legal systems emphasise individual ownership, legal title, and estate planning as tools to manage succession and taxation. These variations are not merely anthropological curiosities—they shape real-world behaviours in acquisition, stewardship, and conflict resolution. *Understanding how cultures pass down property reveals how they conceptualise time, responsibility, and value.*

Consider the case of Germany, where inheritance tax exemptions for passing on family businesses and properties encourage long-term holding. A family-owned building in Berlin may remain under stewardship not because it yields the highest return this year, but because the tax code and social norms reward continuity. Compare that to the United States, where stepped-up basis rules and generous estate tax thresholds allow assets to be transferred with minimal capital gains impact—encouraging intergenerational wealth accumulation, often through dynasty trusts and irrevocable entities. In both contexts, the state participates in shaping intergenerational intent—but in culturally distinct ways. The implication for investors is profound: *thinking generationally requires both legal and cultural fluency.*

But what if you don't have children? What if you don't intend to pass anything down? The temptation might be to dismiss intergenerational strategy as irrelevant. That would be a categorical mistake. Because even without heirs, *you are still building something that outlives you.* Whether that "something" is sold, donated, liquidated, or absorbed by others, it will enter a world you no longer control. Structuring your affairs with care—through charitable trusts, foundations, or community legacies—becomes an act not of inheritance, but of intention. One need not believe in lineage to believe in legacy.

Take, for instance, the growing trend of mission-driven property trusts in cities like Vancouver and Melbourne, where high-net-worth individuals bequeath properties to housing organisations under specific use covenants. These trusts don't merely transfer title—they encode values: affordability, sustainability, dignity. In this way, property becomes a vessel for beliefs, not just assets. A residential building can express your views on community. A commercial site can carry forward your principles around accessibility or design. The mechanism may be legal, but the ambition is philosophical. *Intergenerational thinking is not just about who inherits—it is about what survives.*

This perspective reframes the role of the investor. You are not just acquiring and managing units—you are curating continuity. That includes preparing successors, formal or informal, to understand the assets, their obligations, and their embedded meaning. Too many property portfolios are handed down like forgotten luggage: with no instructions, no context, and no clarity. The result is often mismanagement, neglect, or rapid liquidation. If you intend for a property to remain in a family or organisation, *you must train its next stewards before the transfer, not after.* This means involving heirs in financials, decision-making, legal education, and ethical discussion—well before your name is off the title.

Yet here lies a deeper challenge: *intergenerational transition is not a technical problem—it is a human one.* Family businesses frequently fail in the second generation not because the tax strategy was flawed, but because emotional dynamics—entitlement, resentment, secrecy—were never addressed. Property ownership carries symbolic weight: it can trigger rivalry, hierarchy, or control narratives. The best investors don't just plan legal transfers—they facilitate open dialogue, identify latent tensions, and build consensus around shared intent. This is work that accountants and lawyers cannot do. It demands emotional intelligence, humility, and time.

At the same time, over-planning can also become its own form of rigidity. Not every asset should be preserved indefinitely. Some properties are worth holding; others are better sold. The key is *discernment*, not doctrine. What do you want the next generation to inherit: the building, the income, the responsibility—or the ability to choose among them? A good estate plan defines structure. A great one *preserves agency*. The future should not be a script—it should be a runway.

Indeed, part of thinking generationally is recognising that *you are not the culmination—you are a chapter.* Your work is not to control the ending but to contribute something worthy of continuation. This might mean building resilient portfolios with low debt ratios and clear documentation. It might mean identifying successor leaders in a family office or community foundation. Or it might mean letting go—selling wisely, giving generously, or dissolving outdated holdings that no longer serve their purpose. *Legacy is not what stays—it is what evolves well.*

In practical terms, intergenerational thinking also reorients risk appetite. Many investors in their twenties or thirties think in terms of fast appreciation, leverage, and yield. As portfolios mature—or as one begins to think in decades, not quarters—priorities shift. Stability, reputation, operational simplicity, and long-term tenant relationships begin to outweigh raw ROI. This is not conservatism—it is *architecture.* Think of the difference between flipping properties for margin versus owning a corner shop that anchors a community for forty years. One generates income. The other generates *presence.*

This shift also influences how one approaches debt. While leverage can accelerate growth, it also magnifies risk—and risk that's manageable for a solo investor may be unacceptable in an intergenerational context. Debt that dies with you may not trouble you. Debt that passes to someone else's balance sheet must be reconsidered. The same goes for development timelines, renovation strategies, and legal structuring. Short-termism collapses in the face of legacy.

We return then to a central thesis: *ownership is stewardship.* Whether you hold one unit or one hundred, whether you pass them on to children, tenants, or trustees, what matters is not the scale of the portfolio—but the intention behind its continuity. Have you defined its purpose? Have you documented its logic? Have you prepared others to carry it forward, adapt it, or retire it with wisdom? If not, then what you have built is incomplete—*regardless of its market value.*

To think intergenerationally is to accept the limits of control and the possibility of influence. It is to design not just for profit, but for perpetuity. It is to recognise that your spreadsheet does not end with you. That insight alone demands a recalibration of what it means to be a property investor. Not as an accumulator. Not as a landlord. But as an *architect of continuity.*

The Emotional Side of Legacy:

If all you pass on is a set of deeds, you may leave behind wealth but no meaning. That's the crux of legacy: it's not about what survives you—it's about what endures *because* of you. In real estate, this distinction is frequently lost amid legal structures, asset appraisals, and succession planning. But behind every property lies a story, and behind every portfolio, a philosophy—whether deliberate or not. *The emotional side of legacy is not a sentimental indulgence. It is the most underexamined pillar of estate strategy.* Because long after the spreadsheets have been archived and the tax advantages maximised, what remains is how the people around you understood what you built—and why.

This is not just a matter for families with generational wealth. Even a modest duplex or single rental unit carries narrative weight. How it was acquired, how it was managed, what it funded—these are stories that shape perception, identity, and belonging. The person who grows up knowing their university tuition came from a flat their grandmother bought and cared for sees that property as more than an asset. It becomes a symbol of foresight, sacrifice, and empowerment. Conversely, the heir who inherits a portfolio with no context—no shared history, no known intentions—may treat it with transactional coldness or inherited resentment. *It's not the size of the inheritance that shapes legacy. It's the clarity of the values that come with it.*

Clarity, however, rarely arises by accident. One of the most common oversights in property succession is the failure to narrate the logic behind decisions. Why did you favour single-family homes over commercial assets? Why did you invest in one region and not another? Why did you hold onto a particular building through recessions, vacancies, and capital offers? These are more than tactical choices. They're windows into your thinking. And when articulated—through letters, conversations, or recorded reflections—they provide a template for those who follow. *Without that template, successors may inherit property but not purpose.*

Many investors resist these conversations. They feel too personal, too speculative, or too vulnerable. Yet the failure to speak openly about property philosophy often generates the very confusion and conflict that more transparency could prevent. An heir who believes that a property must be retained "because it's what Dad would have wanted" may hold onto an underperforming asset out of guilt. Another may sell it too quickly, assuming there was no deeper reason for its retention. Silence creates projection. And projection breeds misalignment. *To pass on values is to make your thinking visible before you're absent.*

There is also the matter of emotional context. Property is rarely neutral. It's where holidays happened, businesses were launched, relatives passed away, and children took their first steps. For better or worse, real estate holds memory. A parent's first flat might symbolise escape from poverty. A family's smallholding may represent decades of unity—or conflict. These emotional associations don't show up on balance sheets, but they influence behaviour profoundly. The decision to sell or redevelop isn't just economic—it's moral. *And moral decisions require emotional literacy.*

Consider the case of two siblings inheriting a block of rental units. One views the property as a cash-flow vehicle to optimise. The other sees it as a tribute to their late mother's work ethic and pride. When unspoken, these differing views can escalate into legal disputes or fractured relationships. When discussed, however, they create space for creative compromise: perhaps a partial sale, perhaps a memorialisation of the property's history, perhaps a reinvestment into something that honours the original intent. *Legacy conversations are not just about outcomes—they're about alignment.*

But legacy doesn't have to be passive. One of the most effective ways to instil values is through participation. Involve your children or intended successors in decisions early. Not just in the financial mechanics, but in the moral reasoning. Let them see you choose tenants, review maintenance priorities, negotiate with contractors—not just how you act, but why. This is not about grooming heirs into replicas of yourself. It is about *demystifying the decision-making process*, so that when the responsibility is theirs, they act with confidence—not confusion.

Yet even with perfect communication and alignment, there is no guarantee that your values will be preserved intact. *Legacy is influence, not control.* You cannot force your successors to care about the same things you did. But you can make it easier for them to understand why you cared—and to care thoughtfully in their own way. That is the essence of emotional legacy: it privileges intent over instruction.

One profound yet often neglected consideration is *who gets to inherit the story*, not just the property. Not all heirs are children. Sometimes, it's a long-time tenant, a trusted employee, a community organisation, or a charitable foundation. The emotional side of legacy asks: who truly understands what this property meant—and who is best positioned to carry that meaning forward? The answer may or may not match your bloodline. Legacy, when approached honestly, often challenges assumptions about inheritance, family, and ownership itself.

This brings us to a difficult but necessary point: *not every legacy is positive.* Some property portfolios are built on exploitation, displacement, or environmental harm. Others are wrapped in family dysfunction—where secrecy, control, or favouritism left scars as deep as any financial gain. For such legacies, emotional reckoning is as important as asset planning. Repair, transparency, and even redistribution may be part of a responsible transition. To pass on values is sometimes to *revise them.*

On the other hand, when legacy is built with care, humility, and intentionality, the result transcends property. A portfolio becomes not just an economic engine but an ethical framework. It models patience in a world addicted to speed. It honours craft in a market obsessed with scale. It invites stewardship over consumption. And in doing so, it signals to others—family, partners, communities—that *how you build is just as important as what you build.*

Finally, there is one truth that every thoughtful investor must confront: *you will not be present to explain your legacy when it is most needed.* That's why the emotional dimension must be embedded, not merely appended. It should live in your estate documents, yes—but also in your relationships, your business practices, your recorded reflections. It should be visible in how you treat tenants, how you resolve disputes, and how you model resilience in tough times. *Legacy is not just a message. It is a pattern, repeated consistently enough to become culture.*

What you pass on, in the end, is not the value of your holdings—it's the values embedded in how you held them. And that is the one asset whose appreciation never stops.

Leaving More Than Land:

Ownership, in its rawest form, is not about deeds or titles—it is about meaning. A portfolio of properties, however extensive or modest, is not merely a collection of investments. It is a web of decisions, sacrifices, ambitions, and unspoken values. When you step back from the spreadsheets and yield curves, what remains is the imprint of identity—yours—embedded in brick, mortar, and the spaces you've shaped or preserved. *Real estate is never only about land. It's about what the land represents, to you and those who follow.*

We often associate legacy with scale—the number of units owned, the generational wealth amassed, the net worth headline. But legacy is not measured by square footage or passive income. It's measured by resonance: who remembers, who learns, and who is strengthened by what you leave behind. The temptation in property investing is to focus so tightly on returns that we forget why those returns matter. The final chapter of this book is an invitation to refocus—not away from numbers, but towards the narratives they support.

Consider the child who grows up in a home purchased decades ago with careful planning and modest means. That home becomes more than shelter; it becomes a foundation—emotional, educational, psychological. Or the immigrant family who secures a duplex and rents one half to afford the other. The building itself isn't simply an asset; it's a declaration of agency in a system not designed for them. These stories rarely show up in quarterly cash flow reports. Yet they are the reason the reports exist.

To leave more than land is to think architecturally, but with values, not just materials. It is to ask: What kind of resilience does my portfolio cultivate—for me, for my family, for my community? What kind of behaviour does it reward? What kind of conversations will it spark long after I'm gone? These are not questions accountants can answer, yet they are central to long-term investing. *Wealth becomes wisdom only when you're intentional about the lessons embedded in what you leave behind.*

Different cultures have long understood this. In Japan, the *ie* system viewed land and legacy as indivisible, passed down not just through legal instruments but through rituals of responsibility. In many Indigenous communities, land is not an asset but an ancestor—something you protect, not exploit. Even in European aristocratic estates, the idea of *stewardship*—managing land not for oneself, but as a caretaker for future generations—shapes decisions that prioritise longevity over liquidity. While modern investing tends to be stripped of sentiment, those who last understand that emotional capital is not a weakness—it's leverage.

Yet sentiment alone is not enough. If you intend to leave more than land, you must systematise your values. This means embedding them in your structures—legal, operational, interpersonal. A trust that specifies rental income must support educational scholarships for descendants is one example. A will that grants discounted rent to certain community members is another. These are not theoretical ideals; they are instruments of cultural transmission. Without them, values decay as quickly as under-maintained roofs.

Clarity is essential. Vagueness is the enemy of legacy. Too many investors assume their intentions will be interpreted correctly after they're gone. They won't. A property left to children without guidance becomes a source of friction rather than continuity. "Sell or hold?" becomes a question laced with grief, guilt, and misalignment. The clearer your plan—the rationale behind ownership, the principles guiding its use—the less room there is for confusion or conflict. *A legacy isn't just what you pass on. It's how clearly you communicate why it matters.*

This clarity must extend beyond documents. It must be lived. Tenants notice when a landlord cares. Children absorb unspoken cues about generosity, discipline, ambition. Communities evolve around consistent patterns of engagement or neglect. Whether or not you have heirs in the traditional sense, someone is always watching. A mentee, a neighbour, a sibling, a community organiser—your ownership creates ripples. The question is: are they ones you'd be proud of?

The emotional side of legacy often emerges at the margins of decision-making. Should you sell the property to extract equity, or refinance to reinvest and preserve? Should you renovate with durable materials, knowing it costs more upfront, but lasts longer and reduces tenant turnover? Should you keep a property in a changing neighbourhood because of its historical or cultural relevance, even if the numbers no longer impress? Each choice writes a line in the unwritten memoir of your investment life. *You are always signalling something, even when you're silent.*

Many investors struggle with the tension between pragmatism and purpose. What if your heirs are uninterested? What if your values are misinterpreted? What if your properties become burdens rather than blessings? These are legitimate concerns—and they underscore the need for active communication. A conversation, even a difficult one, is better than a legacy left to guesswork. An ethical will—distinct from a legal one—can provide context. Why you invested, how you made decisions, what mattered most, and what you hope persists. These documents are rarely drafted, but they should be. *Assets without articulation become liabilities of meaning.*

This isn't to argue that every property should be wrapped in sentiment. Some holdings are purely transactional, and that's fine. But if your entire portfolio feels replaceable, you may be missing the deeper potential of real estate as a long-term instrument of impact. The best portfolios reflect both numerical intelligence and narrative intelligence. They earn, but they also teach. They grow, but they also ground. *The investor who thinks this way builds not just equity, but echoes.*

In the end, legacy isn't about scale. It's about signal. What did your decisions say about who you were? What messages did you embed in the spaces you owned? What choices did you make that helped others imagine different possibilities for themselves? Whether or not your name is remembered is irrelevant. What matters is whether your work shaped the conditions under which others could flourish.

Leaving more than land means recognising that real estate is not just a place people live. It's the way they live. And the way you manage, pass on, or relinquish that real estate will say more about you than any investor profile or balance sheet ever could.

Conclusion
Building the Future, One Decision at a Time

There is a quiet illusion that haunts property investing—the idea that there exists a finish line. That if one accumulates enough units, enough equity, enough passive income, a moment of arrival will present itself. Yet any investor with experience knows the truth: there is no summit, only the next ridge. Real estate is not a destination. It is a discipline—continuous, unfinished, and intensely personal.

What you hold—or are in the process of building—is never static. Your portfolio is a mirror of your choices, temperament, and tolerance for risk and resilience. As with any craft of consequence, mastery is not measured in flawless execution but in pattern recognition and subtle adaptation. This final chapter is not a tidy conclusion. It is a mirror: a structured opportunity to evaluate where you have been, what you have internalised, and—most critically—how you will carry that insight forward. Ownership, when pursued thoughtfully, is less a goal than a practice in intentional living.

Eventually, theory softens and spreadsheets fade into lived experience: a tenant surprises you with generosity, a contract you overlooked teaches a costly lesson, a property purchased for the wrong reasons evolves into the right outcome through careful stewardship. These are not footnotes—they are the curriculum. Metrics remain constant, but your relationship to them deepens. Rental yield shifts from arithmetic to philosophy. Cash flow becomes confidence. Maintenance transforms into maturity.

This chapter is not an exercise in self-congratulation. It reframes your journey as an ongoing negotiation between agency and uncertainty. No portfolio, however polished, grants immunity to change. Markets fluctuate. Laws evolve. Tenant expectations shift. Success over decades belongs not to those who never falter, but to those who accumulate more right choices over time by observing, adjusting, and acting with discipline.

Action, even flawed, is the starting point. The myth of the perfect first deal, flawless timing, or seamless renovation paralyses more investors than it inspires. Risk is inevitable; paralysis compounds faster than error. Here, the message is simple: act, imperfectly if necessary, but act with awareness. No spreadsheet can capture the full texture of a living asset. Perfection is an illusion; progress is a deliberate choice.

The pursuit of optimisation carries its own subtle tyranny. Financing terms, tax shelters, emerging markets—they distract and entice. Yet those who sustain momentum understand that advantage lies not in theory, but in follow-through. They recognise their strengths, confront blind spots, and create routines that support consistency. This chapter encourages you to look ahead with actionable focus: which systems require refinement? Which knowledge gaps demand attention? Which professional relationships—advisors, agents, mentors—deserve cultivation?

Equally important: what will you release? Underperforming properties, reactive management habits, outdated notions of success. Growth is seldom additive; it is often subtractive—removing what no longer serves the investor you are becoming.

And perhaps the most pressing question: what are you truly building? Not merely in financial terms, but in human ones. Does your portfolio align with the life you envisaged when first drawn to real estate? Have you sacrificed satisfaction in pursuit of scale, or harmonised ambition with autonomy?

These are strategic, not sentimental, questions. The most effective investors are not those with the largest portfolios. They are those with the clearest sense of purpose, understanding precisely what their assets are meant to achieve—generational security, creative freedom, community impact, or peace of mind. Their decisions are architectural, not reactive. They are constructing a life, not merely a ledger.

The preceding chapters offered a framework, not a formula: analytical, adaptable, and value-anchored thinking. If this book has succeeded, it has sharpened discernment rather than delivered certainty. It has taught you to ask better questions, perceive meaningful patterns, and maintain curiosity amid complexity.

This final chapter is not a curtain call. It is a provocation. Keep your spreadsheets, yes—but alongside them, craft a companion document: the narrative your portfolio tells. Track not only cash flows and cap rates, but convictions—what mattered, what shifted, what endured. For long after loans are repaid and titles transferred, it will not be land that defines your legacy. It will be the clarity, courage, and care with which each decision was made.

This, ultimately, is what it means to build the future—one deliberate choice at a time.

The Practice of Ownership:

Ownership is often romanticised as the endgame—the triumphant result of hard work, sound planning, and ambition rewarded. But those who have lived with property for long enough, those who have repaired the same leaking pipe more than once or renegotiated a contract after years of stability, understand something quieter and more enduring: *ownership is not a destination; it is a discipline.* A practice. One not measured solely by return on investment, but by return on awareness.

The fundamental mistake many first-time investors make is believing that the acquisition of property signals a kind of rest. That once the deal is done and the title is transferred, the work becomes passive. Yet real estate is never truly static. The building ages. The market shifts. Tenants come and go. Governments legislate. Neighbourhoods evolve. And amid all of this, the owner is called not just to react, but to interpret, to adapt, to decide with care. *Ownership demands attentiveness long after the ink dries.*

To frame ownership as a practice is to acknowledge its dual nature: technical and emotional, rational and relational. A seasoned investor knows how to analyse a deal—but also how to hold the uncertainty of it. They understand the calculus of a tax strategy, but also recognise when a decision must be made for values, not just for yield.

This blend of precision and principle is not innate. It is cultivated—through missteps, through mentoring, through patient engagement with the asset and its ecosystem.

There is no fixed curriculum for this work. The lessons come in unpredictable intervals. You learn to trust a contractor only to be let down by one you didn't vet. You manage a tenant relationship with empathy, then find your kindness mistaken for permissiveness. You budget for routine maintenance and discover that "routine" is an optimistic term. These experiences do not signify failure. They signal maturation. Each incident is an invitation to refine your framework—not to panic, not to disengage, but to observe more closely.

This is what makes ownership a mirror. It reflects your tolerance for ambiguity, your patterns of reaction, your willingness to plan and your capacity to pivot. It rewards those who are intellectually alert, emotionally regulated, and logistically grounded. But it does not flatter. It exposes. And for that reason, it is profoundly humanising. Property will humble you if you let it. And through that humility, it will also shape you.

That shaping occurs over time, in cycles rather than milestones. Early in your ownership practice, you may be fixated on monthly profit. Later, your attention may shift to longevity: tenant stability, asset preservation, legacy planning. The lens widens. What once felt transactional becomes relational. You are no longer just collecting rent. You are managing energy, expectations, and entropy. *A seasoned owner sees not just the numbers but the patterns—and begins to manage the rhythm, not just the report.*

It is easy, especially in an age of digitised dashboards and investor apps, to fall into abstraction—to treat properties as code, as data points. But real estate resists full automation. It sits in the world. It moulds to climate, to culture, to the whims of municipal planning boards and the personalities of tenants. It demands presence. And so the practice of ownership becomes, at its best, a kind of mindfulness: *an ongoing negotiation between strategy and stewardship.*

To sustain that negotiation, one must create conditions for reflection. Not just in crises, but as part of regular review. What did this quarter reveal about your assumptions? What decisions drained your attention, and why? Where were you overextended, and where did you move with clarity? These questions are not tangential—they are foundational. Because an ownership model that cannot tolerate reflection will eventually collapse under reactivity.

This chapter is not a call for perfection. In fact, it is the opposite. It is a call to embrace ownership as imperfect by design—a practice shaped by iteration, not completion. The most effective property owners are not those who always get it right. They are those who remain willing to engage, to revise, to keep learning in public. *Mistakes are not disqualifying—they are diagnostic.* They teach you how your systems behave under pressure. They reveal the edges of your competence, so you can reinforce them with skill, not shame.

Moreover, the practice of ownership is not only about asset management—it is about self-management. It requires you to reconcile with risk, to develop patience with process, to resist both panic and hubris. It is an arena in which emotional discipline is as valuable as financial literacy. And it is that emotional discipline that often distinguishes those who endure from those who exit.

You may start this practice with ambition. But to sustain it, you'll need something deeper: *conviction.* Not just that property is a sound investment, but that it is a worthy one. That to be a steward of buildings, land, and living spaces is to contribute something of substance to the human experience. That ownership, done well, is not a solitary climb toward wealth, but a participatory act of responsibility. It connects you to others—to tenants, to tradespeople, to neighbours, to future generations.

None of this is easy. But it is worthwhile. And the rewards are not just measured in income or equity. They are found in moments of calm competence—the repair you anticipated and resolved before it became urgent. The lease clause you rewrote that prevented a conflict. The year-end review in which your properties supported your life, rather than disrupted it. These are not headlines. They are the subtle signs of a practice deepening.

And so, as you continue your work, know that the question is not "Are you done?" The question is "Are you still paying attention?" The practice of ownership will continue to offer its teachings—often at inconvenient times, in unexpected forms. But if you are listening, if you are humble enough to learn and bold enough to act, then you are already participating in something larger than profit. You are cultivating wisdom—through bricks, budgets, and the quiet art of showing up.

Action Without Perfection:

Perfection is seductive. It whispers that if you just read one more book, attend one more seminar, or run one more set of numbers, you'll be ready—invulnerable, flawless, incapable of error. But property investing, like every meaningful form of agency, rewards something else entirely: movement. Not reckless movement, but movement all the same. The real advantage lies not in perfect preparation but in iterative execution. *Progress belongs to those who act before they feel fully prepared, and refine their model through practice rather than premonition.*

The illusion of readiness is especially acute in real estate because of its perceived finality. You sign a contract, allocate significant capital, and enter long-term commitments. It *feels* like you only get one shot. And so, many would-be investors freeze. They overanalyse, postpone, second-guess. They fear the cost of getting it wrong more than they trust the benefit of getting started. But the reality, confirmed by seasoned operators, is this: most success stories in property investing are made not by avoiding mistakes, but by *building resilience around them.*

Consider the early career of any veteran property investor and you'll likely find missteps—purchases made without adequate due diligence, overly optimistic renovation timelines, tenants chosen with insufficient vetting. What distinguishes these individuals is not an unbroken streak of wise decisions, but the ability to *recover, recalibrate, and continue.* They act, assess, learn, and iterate. Perfection isn't part of the cycle. Momentum is.

To embrace action without perfection is not to encourage carelessness. It's to acknowledge that all the knowledge in the world cannot substitute for contextual understanding, which only emerges from doing. A spreadsheet may tell you a deal works; owning the property teaches you *how* it works, *where* it breaks down, and *what* it asks of you as an investor and steward. Theoretical fluency without lived friction is an incomplete education.

In this light, even the so-called failures become instructive. An overpaid purchase in a rising market may still yield equity. A poorly timed renovation can teach resource planning far better than a YouTube tutorial. A challenging tenant might sharpen your communication skills, contract clarity, and emotional regulation. *No action is wasted when paired with rigorous reflection.* The key is to document the decision, diagnose the outcome, and embed the lesson into future operations.

The notion that you can learn to invest by avoiding all error is not just unrealistic—it's intellectually dishonest. Markets are too dynamic, regulations too varied, people too unpredictable. You cannot simulate complexity indefinitely. At some point, you must enter the game and accept that some of your assumptions will be wrong. The question isn't whether you'll make mistakes, but *how you'll absorb and respond to them. That response is your edge.*

This is particularly important for those coming from highly analytical professions—finance, engineering, law—where precision is rewarded and mistakes are penalised. In real estate, too much fixation on precision can paradoxically create risk: deals missed, opportunities stalled, cycles misread. A conservative estimate may keep you safe, but if it keeps you static, it is no longer a tool—it is a tether.

So what does wise action look like in practice? It looks like purchasing your first property with conservative leverage, not waiting until you can afford a portfolio. It means choosing a modest renovation to gain operating experience, not trying to master speculative flipping out of the gate. It means building relationships with tradespeople, agents, and tenants early—not waiting until you have "enough" units to justify delegation. *Action, to be effective, must be proportionate—but also committed.*

Too often, inaction is cloaked in the language of prudence. But prudence without engagement is paralysis. Responsible investing is not defined by the absence of error, but by the presence of *mechanisms to identify and correct those errors quickly*. Insurance, liquidity reserves, mentorship, and mindset form the architecture of that responsiveness. Not caution for its own sake, but *resilience by design*.

Moreover, action without perfection fosters a different kind of confidence—one rooted not in bravado or bravura, but in adaptability. When you've been through enough property cycles, lease disputes, or repair debacles, you stop fearing them. You understand they are features, not bugs, of ownership. Each provides a reference point, a mental model, a playbook for next time. *Perfection makes brittle investors. Experience makes agile ones.*

There is also an ethical dimension to this mindset. The longer you wait to act in pursuit of some idealised readiness, the longer your capital sits idle—unable to house someone, employ someone, or support your own goals. Real estate is not merely an asset class. It's an infrastructure of human living. Every day you postpone participating in that system out of perfectionism is a day of delayed impact. Ownership is responsibility. And responsibility is a form of service—messy, complex, and urgently needed.

Still, this perspective must coexist with critical discernment. Not all action is created equal. Starting small allows you to survive your early mistakes. Choosing properties with intrinsic value cushions against market volatility. Building a margin of safety into your underwriting creates room to manoeuvre. *The goal is not perfection, but intelligent imperfection: flawed steps taken in the direction of competence.*

This is where many books on property investing fall short. They offer formulas, frameworks, and case studies that imply linearity—do A, then B, and C will follow. But your real estate practice will not be linear. It will lurch, backtrack, accelerate, and recalibrate. You may make a brilliant acquisition followed by a mediocre one. You might misjudge a neighbourhood, then spot a sleeper. The lesson is not to avoid missteps, but to *build rhythm amid inconsistency.*

And that rhythm, over time, becomes your methodology. Not someone else's checklist, but your own evolving system—built from fieldwork, fortified by introspection, and tuned to your strengths, values, and tolerance. It is this system, not any single decision, that defines your long-term success.

So the call here is not simply to act. It is to *act with integrity, with learning in mind, and with structures in place to support you when—not if—you miss the mark.* Real estate, at its best, is not a static portfolio but a growing body of insight. It is cultivated through engagement, not contemplation. Through risk, not rhetoric.

Ultimately, the question is not "Are you ready?" but "Are you willing to learn by doing?" If the answer is yes, then your readiness is irrelevant. The work begins where the certainty ends. And what emerges is not a perfect investor, but a practicing one. One who acts, iterates, and endures.

Designing Your Next Decade:

The decisions that matter most often unfold in the quiet spaces between the milestones—those moments when you're not buying, selling, or renovating, but considering what's next. It's in these intervals that a real estate investor becomes something more than an opportunist or technician: a strategist, a builder of futures. The next decade won't be shaped by a single deal, but by a series of deliberate steps that compound, interlock, and echo. To design it wisely, you must think in both architecture and time.

This isn't about ten-year plans carved in granite. The idea of scripting your next decade with mechanical precision misunderstands the nature of both markets and life. But neither is it a freefall into improvisation. What's needed is a dynamic framework—one that evolves with you, yet keeps your momentum tethered to meaning. It requires not only financial literacy but also emotional clarity: a clear understanding of what you're solving for, beyond yield percentages and capital gains.

Start by considering this: What story do you want your portfolio to tell ten years from now? Not just in net worth, but in function. Do your properties make life easier or more chaotic? Are they helping you transition into the roles you want—whether as a passive investor, a philanthropist, a mentor, or simply someone who sleeps better at night knowing their money is working quietly, and well?

In real terms, this means setting up a layered structure of actions—short-term, medium-term, and long-term—while resisting the illusion that one timeline is more important than the others. For example, your short-term actions might include refinancing to increase cash flow, upgrading neglected infrastructure, or securing more tax-efficient ownership vehicles. These moves buy you time, liquidity, and optionality—currency you'll need for your medium-term shifts, such as repositioning your portfolio around lifestyle changes or new geographic markets. The long-term arc then emerges not from prediction, but from accumulated alignment. Over ten years, small but thoughtful decisions mature into strategic advantage.

But alignment doesn't happen by accident. It begins with distinguishing between activity and progress. Many investors confuse the former for the latter—renovating units, chasing listings, tweaking spreadsheets. But activity untethered from purpose is just professional inertia. Designing your next decade means asking questions that are inconvenient, sometimes uncomfortable: Why do I own what I own? Does it still serve me, or do I serve it? What am I optimising for now—cash flow, control, freedom, impact?

These questions aren't rhetorical. They're design tools. And they point to a foundational shift that seasoned investors eventually make: from optimisation to orientation. In your early years, you chase ROI with almost religious fervour. But as the portfolio grows, as life complicates and priorities shift, ROI alone becomes an insufficient compass. You begin to orient instead around *resilience*—of income, of relationships, of time. You measure your assets not only by what they generate, but by what they protect: your schedule, your sanity, your sovereignty.

This brings us to a fundamental insight: a well-designed decade integrates more than assets—it integrates identity. Who are you becoming as an investor, and what does that version of you need from your holdings? For some, this means moving from hands-on property management to leveraged systems. For others, it means exiting legacy properties that no longer align with where life is headed. And for many, it involves a deeper shift—from being the hero of the portfolio to being its steward. You don't need to control every variable. You need to understand what matters, who you can trust, and where you add irreplaceable value.

Consider the role of liquidity in this context. It's fashionable in property circles to equate illiquidity with commitment, to romanticise long holds as the ultimate badge of honour. But liquidity is not weakness—it's wisdom, if strategically preserved. A portion of your next decade's success will depend not just on your holdings but on your holdings' *flexibility*. Can they be sold, refinanced, or restructured if your personal or market conditions shift? Designing forward means preserving that optionality without surrendering discipline.

Likewise, don't underestimate the emotional architecture of the next ten years. Boredom, fear, distraction—these are not incidental. They shape decisions as surely as interest rates and tax codes. Build systems that counter them: accountability partners, quarterly reviews, written investment theses for each property. Treat these habits as seriously as you treat due diligence. Ten years of clear-headedness beats ten years of compulsive tinkering.

At the macro level, consider where the world is heading. Are you positioning yourself in areas of economic vitality, demographic growth, and regulatory sanity? Are you future-proofing your assets against climate volatility, technological disruption, and policy whiplash? Ten years is enough time for small advantages to snowball—and for blind spots to metastasize. The global property map will not look the same in 2035 as it does today. Build accordingly.

Then there's the matter of legacy. Not the romanticised version that shows up in glossy estate-planning brochures, but the quieter kind—

habits of transparency, systems that others can inherit without unraveling, records that aren't locked in your head. Whether you intend to pass your portfolio to children, charities, or business partners, designing your next decade should involve creating assets that are legible, teachable, and transferable.

Finally, design with a healthy respect for imperfection. Not everything will unfold on schedule. Some decisions will haunt you before they help you. Markets will defy logic. Tenants will surprise you. Life will intervene. But progress is not linear, and clarity is not static. Designing a decade is less about dictating outcomes and more about cultivating conditions—so that when the right opportunity arrives, you're ready not just financially, but philosophically.

The investor who succeeds over ten years isn't necessarily the one with the highest returns. It's the one whose decisions became *increasingly coherent*, increasingly aligned with who they are and what they value. They didn't just build assets—they built judgement. And that is what endures.

Final Reflection: What Are You Really Building?

Real estate, at its surface, is measured in concrete and square metres. Yet over time, the deeper you go into ownership, management, and legacy, the more you realise this: what you're truly constructing is not simply a portfolio—it's a philosophy. Each property acquired, improved, or sold reflects a series of decisions that reveal your beliefs about risk, security, responsibility, and the future. That truth is easy to miss when focus narrows to interest rates and rental yields, but in the final analysis, the most profound question in property investing is not how much you've acquired—it's why you've acquired it at all.

One of the least discussed yet most impactful forces in long-term ownership is alignment—between your values and your ventures. It's entirely possible to build a technically successful portfolio that leaves you feeling ethically conflicted, emotionally drained, or personally disconnected. The market might reward you with capital gains, yet offer no affirmation that what you're building aligns with who you are. That disconnect, if left unexamined, tends to compound—not just financially, but psychologically. It shows up in strained relationships, burned-out decision-making, or portfolios that outgrow their purpose. It is this misalignment—subtle yet potent—that often causes investors to feel disillusioned despite financial success. Real estate, like any long game, ultimately becomes an expression of the self.

This is why intentionality must be treated not as a luxury but as a form of strategy. Investors are taught to run the numbers, but few are taught to interrogate their motivations. Ask yourself: Are you accumulating property to prove something to others? To secure personal freedom? To preserve wealth across generations? To enable philanthropic ambitions? To stabilise your family? Your answers matter, because they influence the shape of your portfolio and the stress you endure to maintain it. A landlord who values autonomy might structure their holdings radically differently than someone who values legacy or liquidity. And those distinctions ripple through every practical choice—from how aggressively to leverage, to what markets to enter, to when to delegate management.

Consider the emotional architecture of a portfolio. A flat in an urban high-rise might symbolise independence or upward mobility. A countryside cottage, preservation and tradition. A multifamily development might signify ambition, while a trust-held estate might reflect intergenerational stewardship. The bricks are the same. The meanings are not. The properties we hold inevitably become metaphors for the lives we lead, and those metaphors grow heavier as time passes. It is no small matter to realise that your assets do not just provide for your life—they begin to shape it.

Many investors reach a point—often after a decade or two—where they realise they've become custodians of structures they no longer fully understand. The properties remain profitable, but their original purpose has evaporated. Perhaps they were acquired during a phase of life now long past: when raising children, when starting over, when chasing financial independence. The question that arises isn't, "Should I sell?" but rather, "What role does this asset play in my life now?" And if that role is unclear or irrelevant, a form of strategic entropy sets in. Maintenance becomes a burden, tax planning turns reactive, and decision-making is fuelled by inertia rather than clarity. This is the real cost of building without a blueprint of meaning.

To avoid this drift, the most sophisticated investors design feedback loops—not just for market conditions, but for personal alignment. They make time to regularly re-articulate their goals, revisit their assumptions, and evaluate their holdings against more than spreadsheets. A quarterly review of rental income means little if the properties no longer reflect your ethics, priorities, or plans. And that process needn't be sentimental. It is, in fact, a form of governance—an internal system of checks and balances that ensures your property investments remain assets, not liabilities, to the life you want to live.

For those without heirs, this reflection takes on a different texture. If no one is standing in line to inherit what you've built, then the meaning must come from elsewhere: perhaps from the security it affords, the lives it houses, or the causes it funds. In such cases, the traditional narrative of legacy gives way to a broader notion of contribution. A portfolio might be structured to support artists, single parents, refugees, or ecological restoration. The buildings don't change, but their social utility does—and with that shift comes a richer sense of purpose. You are no longer just preserving wealth; you are directing energy.

Cultural context adds another layer. In some societies, property is passed down with sacred significance, carrying the weight of familial honour and collective memory. In others, it's seen as a personal asset to be liquidated, leveraged, or diversified at will. Understanding your own cultural inheritance—and whether it fits the life you wish to lead—is essential. Too often, investors unconsciously follow patterns inherited from their upbringing, community, or peers without ever interrogating their fit. But unexamined tradition is no more strategic than reckless innovation. Whether you're replicating your parents' model or rebelling against it, do so consciously.

The philosophical layer of ownership becomes most potent when paired with humility. No matter how well-structured, every portfolio is an experiment. Markets shift. Tenants change. Health declines. Laws evolve. Your own preferences may flip entirely. The best investors are not those who cling to certainty, but those who treat property as a process of constant learning. They understand that wisdom in real estate is not measured by perfect foresight but by the quality of your reflection. That includes learning from mistakes, rebalancing expectations, and redefining success across stages of life.

This final reflection, then, is not about grand declarations. It is about daily posture. Do your investment choices move you closer to a life of dignity, autonomy, contribution, and alignment? Or do they entrench you in stress, resentment, or confusion? The answer will not come from your accountant. It will not be revealed by the market. It will not appear in a headline. It will come from within—usually quietly, and only after you've made space to ask.

What you are really building is not just net worth. You are building a worldview. You are shaping the way you respond to uncertainty, the kind of opportunities you create for others, the stories your children—or your community—will tell about your impact. Whether you own a single rental flat or a transnational portfolio, the question remains the same: What values are embedded in the walls you hold title to? If you don't know, then the project is incomplete.

In real estate, as in life, ownership is not simply a state of possession. It is a form of participation. You are a participant in systems of housing, justice, capital, and culture. The homes you buy and rent influence the wellbeing of strangers, the structure of neighbourhoods, the price of access. That reality doesn't disappear with legal separation or market abstraction. The final test of stewardship is not how many assets you control, but whether you have used your control wisely.

So pause. Reframe. Return to the foundational inquiry that most investors skip in their haste to acquire: What are you really building—and is it worthy of your time, talent, and legacy?

That is the question that will follow you long after the mortgage is paid.

About the Author

Elias Wren writes about the intersection of value, meaning, and long-term thinking in an age of instant everything. After years of navigating real estate markets not just as an investor but as a student of people, places, and patterns, Elias brings a uniquely grounded perspective to wealth-building. His passion lies in helping everyday individuals reclaim power in their financial lives—without compromising their values or identities. Elias believes that investing is not just a financial act, but a personal philosophy—a way to participate in shaping the future with clarity, intention, and care. His work is known for its quiet depth, emotional honesty, and unapologetic realism.

www.ingramcontent.com/pod-product-compliance
Lightning Source LLC
Chambersburg PA
CBHW020240250926
51848CB00007BA/428
9789371778688